W9-AKE-222

*745.9,
T   5774
Tangye, Enid
Flowers for all occasions

EAU CLAIRE DISTRICT LIBRARY

FLOWERS

for all occasions

635.9
J.

FLOWERS

for all occasions

ENID TANGYE

WITHDRAWN

HAWTHORN BOOKS, INC. *Publishers* NEW YORK

EAU CLAIRE DISTRICT LIBRARY

5774

73749

Copyright © Enid Tangye, 1964. Copyright under International and Pan-American Copyright Conventions. All rights reserved, including the right to reproduce this book, or portions thereof, in any form, except for the inclusion of brief quotations in a review. All inquiries should be addressed to Hawthorn Books, Inc., 70 Fifth Avenue, New York City 10011. This book was printed in Great Britain and originally published in 1964 by Evans Brothers Limited, Montague House, Russell Square, London, W.C.1. Library of Congress Catalogue Card Number: 66–14517.

May, 1966

Printed in England
3709

Contents

Illustrations in black and white

Illustrations in colour

All the illustrations were arranged by the author and photographed by E. Howard Symmons, F.R.P.S.
The diagrams were prepared by the author and Rachel Sarrieddine.

To Colin, without whose encouragement
this book could not have been written

I. Gathered Flowers

So much has been written in recent years on the topic of flower arrangement that it might well be felt that there is little left to be said. This, in a sense, is true, but there is always a difference in the individual approach to any specific subject and, as time passes, changes are evolved by experiment (often governed by fashion), so that there is a continuous evolution even in a matter as well known as this.

Flowers have been one of the joys of my life and I have always felt that they were made for the delight of those who rarely see them growing just as much as for those who take pleasure in their cultivation.

If the purpose of this book is mainly to extol the use of flowers for decorative purposes indoors, it is because I have been guided throughout its preparation by the belief that gathered flowers bring increasing pleasure to so many of us. In fact, I think people are more aware of flowers now than ever before, principally because they know more about them, and I cannot believe that the extraordinary interest taken in flower arrangement could have reached its present dimensions if the medium used had not given such universal pleasure. The perfection of the structure of flowers is a challenge to our artistry and, in the development of their arrangement indoors, creative talents have been discovered in many people who would otherwise have been unaware that they possessed them.

Any popular movement evokes criticism, and flower arrangement, as such, is no exception. Nevertheless its appeal has been almost world-wide and I feel it is the flowers themselves which have magnetically drawn together people from every walk of life. For generations gardeners have shared a keen interest in their chosen subject, and now there is an ever-increasing company of people who have become interested in flowers even though, through force of circumstances, they may possess no garden of

9

their own. I feel that this is something that should be encouraged to the utmost. A new artistic interest has been born in the last few decades which has added immeasurably to the beauty of our homes.

For the development of this interest we must pay tribute to the late Constance Spry, who was the first to open our eyes to the potentialities of flower decoration in this country as we know it now. Many others have followed in her footsteps, or have developed new ideas and a different approach to the fundamental lines of flower arrangement, but we should remember with gratitude that she was the first to pioneer the arrangement of flowers as an integral part of interior decoration, and her impeccable good taste has been a target to which many, including myself, have aspired.

Fashions in flower arrangement change as they do with everything else and, although nothing can progress without new ideas, I think the present should benefit from the past, having due regard to its values which can be used as stepping-stones to improvement. Where flowers are concerned it would be wise, perhaps, to bear in mind that our aim should be to maintain their initial beauty. It is, unfortunately, only too easy to defeat this aim in our efforts to be different, original or clever, since flowers, however lovely in themselves, can look oddly grotesque if arranged in a manner out of sympathy with their natural habits of growth.

A truly satisfying arrangement of flowers is dependent, to my mind, mainly on two things: firstly, a flowing and natural design in which no conflicting detail, either in colour blending or a seemingly broken line, upsets the visual balance, and secondly, the imaginative portrayal of individual flowers which comes from an appreciation of the personalities of the flowers themselves.

In order to emphasize the real beauty of flowers in decoration it is necessary to observe and study them and, so to speak, 'get the feel of them' so that eventually we can depict them in a manner consistent with their natural habits and intrinsic qualities. An arrangement in which the flowers, leaves or branches flow out from a centre of gravity in their right proportions, as they do in growth, can appear almost untouched by hand. I have never felt that cut flowers will look well, or last, if induced to follow lines unrelated to their natural inclinations, so the purpose of this book is to try to show, wherever possible, a manner of arrangement whereby gathered flowers can retain indoors something of their original character.

Although the arrangement of flowers in our homes and in public places has become, for many, an acquired art which requires practice to attain proficiency, it would be a pity if this should discourage those who have neither the time nor the opportunity to study flower arrangement from having flowers around them. The joy of flowers is for everyone. Those who have no time to 'do the flowers' in the accepted sense can nevertheless make the most of what is available by giving a thought to the care of flowers and to the kind of vase in which to put them. A single stem can reach perfection if the proportion of flower to vase is correct. A tight bunch of brilliant flowers (still, if you like, 'bunched' from the florist) can lighten a room amazingly when placed solidly in a jar, and many gathered flowers will take their own graceful shape, with no necessity for their arrangement, in the right-sized vase.

I do not feel that there should be such a thing as a 'set piece' in flower arrangement. Every group is something new, evolved by the personal interpretation of the decorator from the material available, in which preferences will show, both in style and in the emphasis placed on favourite flowers. The suggestions which are given in the following pages are intended, therefore, merely as patterns to simplify initial efforts and should not be regarded as a basis for all future work. Anyone who has a love of flowers, and an interest in their arrangement indoors, should approach the subject in her own way, helped in the first place by the lessons learned by those of longer experience. And there is such a wealth of example behind us now that we should be able to draw on the best from all schools of thought to suit our individual requirements.

I have found that even a remotely satisfying arrangement of flowers will lead one onward to new ideas and encourage one to strive for the perfection which is, somehow, always just round the corner. But even if satisfaction is very rarely achieved, the eye becomes increasingly observant and the mind more perceptive to beauty, so that life, in consequence, is filled with an extra interest and richness that might otherwise have passed one by.

2. Some General Principles of Flower Arrangement

It would, I think, be very difficult to define exactly what constitutes the perfect arrangement of flowers. The charm of the design, the proper blending of colour and the suitability of the flowers to their background are not in themselves generally sufficient to be entirely arresting. It is, more probably, a sensitivity in the mind and hands of the arranger that can imbue the arrangement with the natural characteristics of the flowers themselves. This is something intangible, which cannot be taught by rules, but there are certain established methods which can be helpful to the inexperienced in that they provide a basis for the later development of a personal style.

The purpose of the following suggestions is to indicate the easiest way to achieve certain effects in flower arrangement and to prolong the lives of the flowers for as long as possible.

Gathering the flowers

Few people seem to realize that it is as important to gather flowers judiciously from the garden as it is to buy them economically from the shop or market. An over-abundance of material invariably results in damaged flowers, and ravages plants and shrubs unnecessarily. When possible it is advisable to gather the material for each specific group separately rather than to collect a heterogeneous mass in anticipation that it may be useful. I do not wish to suggest by this that one should approach the garden with set ideas on exactly what is required, as the blossoming of some particular flower can entirely alter previously laid plans and one's mind should always be open to surprise and delight. With practice, however, it is possible, and preferable, to gather the correct amount for each arrangement by assembling the flowers in the hand in the manner the arrangement is envisaged.

As a counsel of perfection it is best to pick the flowers the evening before they are required and to place them in water even before attention is given to their individual requirements. If this is not possible it is nevertheless advisable to avoid picking during the hottest part of the day, and under no condition should flowers be left lying about unprotected from the sun. On occasions I pick directly into a can of water, as some particularly temperamental types would otherwise wilt even under the most careful orthodox treatment. Scissors and secateurs should be kept sharp, as blunt ones can bruise and tear delicate stems.

The care of flowers

Flowers from a garden or from a shop generally require the same treatment, as we cannot be sure that bought flowers have been correctly conditioned. Water is the main requirement and they need several hours, preferably overnight, in water deep enough to cover half to three-quarters of their stems. The reason for this, which is not always understood, is that if the stems can absorb moisture for their whole length initially, they will retain it to feed the flower heads even if only a few inches are under water in the final arrangement. Even an hour in deep water (which should be tepid in winter) is better than none at all.

Sufficient pails should be ready before the picking is begun, as the less delay there is between cutting the flowers and placing them in water the less likelihood there is of loss or damage. Overcrowding should be avoided in case delicate heads become entangled and, where a large quantity is required, it is advisable to have a separate pail for each type of flower or, alternatively, for the material for each specific group if it has been gathered in that way.

Any leaves that could lie beneath the surface of the water should be removed first of all and the stems recut. Hard-wooded flowers, such as roses or chrysanthemums, should have their stems split for about one inch from the bottom and either peeled at the base or bruised with, preferably, a wooden mallet. Heavy stems of blossom, shrubs or foliage require the bases hammered, and in the case of blossom and some shrubs most of the heavier leaves should be removed. Lilac and philadelphus will last much longer if partially stripped of leaves, as the water absorbed into the stems can then support the flowers more adequately.

Certain hollow-stemmed flowers, such as lupins and dahlias, and those that 'bleed', like poppies and poinsettias, will often last longer if the tips of their stems are held for a few seconds in a pan containing an inch or two of boiling water before they are given the usual long drink. The heads should be protected from any damage by steam but, as the whole procedure is rather involved, I rarely use it myself except for very precious flowers. Alternatively, the tips of the stems can be sealed by singeing for a few seconds under a flame. Hot water itself is a great reviver. Many drooping flowers will pick up miraculously if immersed for a time in really hot water, but care must be taken to remove leaves beneath the water-level and room should be left for any steam to escape.

Long-stemmed shop roses benefit from being rolled in paper, reaching beyond their total length, prior to their conditioning drink, as this prevents their heads from drooping before the water is absorbed. This treatment can be repeated if the roses show signs of flagging when subjected to central heating. It is best if all roses are de-thorned before they are used in arrangements, as thorn pricks are painful. Tulips, which have a wayward habit of flowing in all directions when cut, also benefit from a preliminary roll in paper while immersed in deep water, as this induces them to straighten, **at** least temporarily.

Some flowers, like hydrangeas, occasionally need to absorb moisture through their faces as well as through their stems, and if a dejected-looking head is placed face down in water for a time it will generally revive completely. Violets too will freshen up amazingly if they are covered with damp tissue paper.

Sometimes a particular flower will droop for no accountable reason after only a short time in a vase. This may be caused by an air lock in the stem, and a repetition of the conditioning treatment, together with the removal of half an inch off the stem, will more often than not completely revive it.

Stimulants for flowers

Ranging from the old adage of aspirin in the water to the various stimulants now on the market for the purpose of aiding the prolongation of the life of cut flowers there is much to be found that is useful. I am inclined to try anything that seems reasonable on the assumption that as fertilizers help growing flowers, so should certain chemicals intensify the beauty and prolong the life of cut flowers. But their use is limited in that they provide no alternative to the foregoing suggestions on the care of flowers.

Filling up vases

However much we may adhere to rules pertaining to the care of flowers prior to their arrangement in a vase, our efforts will be fruitless if we neglect their needs thereafter. Flowers cannot live without moisture and light, and it is a strangely contradictory fact that after all the trouble taken over their arrangement they die all too often, long before their time, owing to disinterest in their subsequent requirements.

Vases should be only partially filled with water before an arrangement is begun because the insertion of flowers will cause the level to rise and a too-full vase can result in an unfortunate overflow with consequent damage to table surfaces. When the arrangement is completed the vase should be filled to the brim, and it is often necessary to repeat this a few hours later as flowers and foliages drink copiously during their first day in a vase. According to the time of year or the room temperature, vases should be 'topped up' at least once a day thereafter. It is often advisable to take a later look at a vase after its final filling up, as certain leaves which are soft and slightly 'hairy' will absorb too much moisture and, when saturated, will start siphoning the water out again. It is a wise precaution to dry thoroughly any leaves which may offend in this way before insertion into the vase, particular attention being given to the underside of the leaf.

Provided the vases are kept well filled it is not necessarily beneficial to move the flowers periodically to a cool place. Indeed the reverse is generally the case, as few but the most professionally arranged groups could retain their shape with constant moving around. Some easily handled small arrangements do benefit occasionally from a rest in a cool place, and particularly delicate flowers, such as Lenten roses, need at times not only a change in temperature but renewed immersion in warm water if their lives are to be prolonged to the utmost.

15

'FANTASY' FREESIAS

This exquisite double freesia, so aptly called 'Fantasy', is truly a freesia beyond one's wildest dreams! It has taken, I am told, nearly twenty years to perfect and only recently has it become available in any quantity. Still limited to a brief season, unlike other freesias which are gradually (and perhaps rather regrettably) becoming, like chrysanthemums, perpetual flowers, 'Fantasy' are borne on long, sturdy stems so that the variety is not only bigger and less fragile than others of its species but its lasting qualities are considerably longer.

Despite the development in size the fragrant scent of freesias remains unspoiled which is a great tribute to the grower as, though many flowers can be increased both in form and beauty, the haunting charm of scent is lost too often.

Deep cream is an unusual colour among flowers but these freesias are entirely this with no hint of yellow. I chose, therefore, to use as foliage the last of the little kale leaves as many had assumed by March just the same ivory tone. The cream tinted ivy is known as 'Canary Island' ivy.

The flowers and leaves were inserted into a dampened block of Oasis in much the same pattern as shown in the illustrations between pages 24 and 25.

LENTEN ROSES WITH COLOURED FOLIAGES

The quiet colours in this small arrangement of Lenten roses may not be to everyone's taste. Such a shadowy combination could soon be forgotten amid the more colourful flowers which follow on their heels, but for those who find appeal in muted tones, as I do, these shaded flowers and foliages have undoubted charm.

Unlike the Christmas rose (*H. niger*), these later hellebores are not easy flowers to use in decoration as their lasting powers are variable, particularly among the darker types. For the sake of their rounded outline, rare among flowers at this time of year, and of their graceful manner of growth it is worth persevering with methods to maintain their life for as long as possible. They benefit from the hot-water treatment when first brought indoors and are best left in a cool, moist place during the period of their initial long drink. If, despite this care, they tend to soften and go limp in heated rooms, it is worth re-cutting the stems and repeating the conditioning treatment when, in all probability, they will completely recover.

The hellebores illustrated here, *H. orientalis*, are among the most difficult to keep indoors but all, except one deep purple flower, lasted undisturbed for several days despite the fact that they were subjected to the extra heat of photography lights. The fact that these were gathered from well-established roots probably accounted for their stamina, as the degree of maturity reached by a plant has considerable effect on the lasting powers of the flowers or leaves cut from it.

The minute scented flowers of *Jasminum polyanthum*, together with the different coloured foliages, seemed suitable companions for this small group of rather subtle tones. Foliage is always important either as a foil to brighter colours or as an additional interest to a group and, in this arrangement, it was as much a part of the design as were the flowers. The bright silver *Senecio leucostachys*, which formed three of the outline stems, has deeply cut leaves on long flexible stems and has, for me, more elegance than the rather similar *Senecio cineraria* (also called *Cineraria maritima*) which is more bushy in growth. The ivy-leaved *Pelargonium peltatum* added solidity to the centre, while the lighter green and white *Pelargonium crispum* 'Variegatum' together with the *Senecio leucostachys* helped to soften the outline.

17

Preparation of vases

Whatever means are adopted the adequate preparation of vases beforehand is of the greatest importance. In my experience wire-netting is the best medium for holding flowers in place in all classical-shaped vases. A two-inch mesh, pliable 19-gauge, is the most generally useful and can be bought in an eighteen-inch width. A medium-sized vase will require between half and three-quarters of a yard, but the amount is very much a matter of personal taste. It should be crumpled up in such a manner that it reaches the base of the vase but that outside pieces are available to clip over the sides; it should be firmly immovable and can be tied to handles, or around the vase, for extra safety. For really big arrangements, such as church groups, a heavier 17- or 18-gauge wire-netting is advisable as it will remain immovable under the weight of water-filled tubes or heavy branches. A white plastic wire-netting has recently been designed for the purpose of aiding flower arranging and can be bought in suitable lengths at many flower shops. It has the advantage of lasting almost indefinitely and does not scratch the inside of vases as ordinary wire can do. In glass vases the wire must not be allowed to show, and about three thicknesses should be fitted over the top instead of being crumpled up inside.

Heavy metal pin-holders are useful for line arrangements in shallow troughs or dishes, as they hold the main stems securely. But even with these I use a little wire-netting, as an arrangement consisting solely of impaled flowers lacks all softness and naturalness. It is occasionally advisable to tether the pin-holder to the dish with the aid of a little Plasticine, as it can become unbalanced with the weight of branches.

Florapak, which is a florists' commodity procurable at most flower shops, is useful for many small arrangements such as baskets or vases of flowers which are to be delivered as presents, and for table decorations which may have to be moved from place to place. It should be remembered, however, that Florapak should be prepared the day before it is required, as time is necessary for water to be properly absorbed before the Florapak can be firmly pressed and wedged into the vase. For demonstration and exhibition purposes Oasis, and the more recently introduced Fomos, are useful, as both absorb water like a sponge and remain for a time so firm and solid that flower stems can be inserted at all angles. They are particularly useful in shallow containers as they retain their shape, whereas Florapak, which crumbles, must be contained within a vase.

When valuable silver and glass vases are used it is wise to protect the inner surfaces from scratches before using any device to support the flowers. Glass can be adequately protected, and still maintain its trans-parency, by an inside lining of polythene. Tin-foil is a better medium for silver as it can be cut to shape and fitted over the edges of wide vases such as silver cake baskets or rose bowls.

Proportions

Rules and regulations seem inappropriate where flowers are concerned and I hesitate to advocate their use in case they should be given too much importance. On the other hand they can be useful in regard to the main problems of line and balance, as some basic principles apply to most designs and provide a foundation which can help to simplify the first steps in any arrangement.

To my mind, the perfect flower arrangement should be completely satisfying to the eye. This visual perfection is based, very largely, on the correct proportion between the vase and the flowers it contains and the proper balance of the design. One of the most usual errors is to have a vase too big for its surroundings and the flowers available. Another is to start the outline either too far back, or too far forward, in the vase so that the arrangement is unbalanced from the start.

Flowers in their natural state have a certain strength about them, and a group will rise with vigour and grace from a single source. Therefore, if we wish to simulate this natural effect in our arrangements, we too should have a positive strong line as the basis of our designs. Any group that stems from a central point, whether it is to be tall or long and low, requires a flexible backbone, like the spine in a human body, which will indicate the design and be the pivot of the whole arrangement. Similarly, although the 'spine' in modern line designs will often rise from the side rather than from the centre of the receptacle, the subsidiary stems should still flow out from the same source, thereby giving an effect of strength and growth.

TRADITIONAL DESIGNS

The following proportions are offered as a guide for some of the most commonly used traditional designs. It is not intended that they should be taken too literally, as every type of arrangement varies according to its surroundings and also to the personal taste of the arranger.

The triangular or fan-shaped arrangement

This type of arrangement, which is perhaps the most commonly used of all, is seen from the front and sides only and, in general principle, it is usual for the tallest stem to be one and a half times the total height of the vase. The main side stems should then extend in almost the same proportion, and a forward central stem should be about a third of this length. It may simplify matters if the basic stems are tabulated and described in detail. As I see it, the tallest (which we will call A) should be the spine of the arrangement and should govern the design. It should be inserted firmly in an almost central position in line with the rear wall of the stem of the vase. I am aware that it is usual to place this stem rather farther back but I have found that a far more natural effect is gained if the arrangement flows from an almost completely central axis. The two main side stems (B and C) should now be inserted equally firmly horizontally in a line meeting just behind A but relative to each other. Provided these stems are kept beneath the water-level they can drink in a lateral position just as well as in a vertical one.

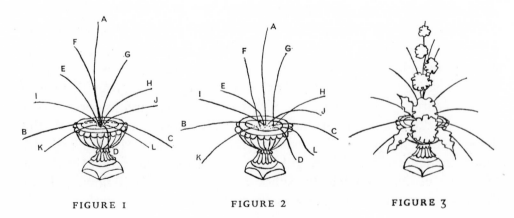

FIGURE I   FIGURE 2   FIGURE 3

The forward stem (D) indicates depth and should be placed at right angles to A, but should spill slightly downwards over the rim of the vase. Now that the basic lines are indicated the filling-in can begin. Four more stems of varying lengths (E to H) are added to form a fan-shaped outline, but they should come as nearly as possible from the same point as A. Then two more horizontal stems (I and J) are inserted, which can follow the lines of B and C but should tip slightly backward for balance. In order that the forward stem should be united with the side ones two further stems (K and L) are added in front of B and C, and these should spill downwards. (These steps are illustrated in Figure 1.)

It is important, at this point, to make certain that those lines which indicate the design are relative to each other or the visual balance will be upset. In Figure 2 the same number of stems are shown arranged in a manner where they are neither relative to each other nor come from a central point. The correct placing of the initial stems forms a basis for lines of similar flowers, and drifts of colour, which are far more effective than a haphazard dotting about of different types. It requires only a little practice before a seemingly broken line is immediately discernible.

Attention should now be given to depth, which has already been indicated by D. About four or five stems (although this depends on the type available) should be inserted between A and D at an angle which permits them to tip forward and form a swelling curve, but this must be uneven in depth or the profile will be too symmetrical. In most arrangements of mixed flowers an indication of weight is necessary for proper balance, so that larger leaves or open-faced flowers can be inserted centrally and slightly behind the curve, some of them being placed quite low in the vase. (See Figure 3.) Any remaining spaces should be filled in by stems which flow from the same axis as the central or side ones, and a stem or two of foliage should be inserted at a slightly backward angle behind A to provide balance and to fill in the back of the vase. The foregoing positions apply to arrangements of one type of flowers just as well as to mixed arrangements, but where there is a choice of different material it is best to use pointed or slender flowers and foliage for the outline and open-faced flowers for the curving middle, keeping the most important flower or flowers to form a focal point.

Arrangements viewed from all sides: the all-round arrangement

This, as its name implies, is a symmetrical design and is most effective as the focal point in a room if placed on a central table, or on top of a font as a welcoming group for a wedding service or, on a small scale, as a dinner-table decoration. It is not, however, an easy design to do successfully as it requires a considerable number of flowers and care must be taken to avoid heaviness.

Height cannot be measured here in relation to the vase, as it may be a flat bowl, but, whatever size is required, it should be similar in height and width. For instance, if the tallest upright stem (A) is twelve inches, then the four lateral ones (B to E) should be the same length and should be placed at right angles to the vertical stem like the four points of a compass. (Figure 4.) Four more stems (F to I) are placed horizontally in the centre of the 'triangles' formed by the first ones but should be slightly shorter in length. (Figure 5.)

The framework is now complete in that height and width all round are established, and it remains for the vertical stem to be united with the laterals to form a pleasant rounded shape. This can be done in a number of ways, the most popular of which is to complete one side first and then repeat the process on the opposite side. Occasionally, however, this can have the effect of two pieces being stuck together, as flowers or colours do not flow through to the whole extent of their visual line. The simplest method is, perhaps, to insert first the stems which join A to the four compass points, because these form the main outline and should be composed of the same type of foliage or flowers. About six stems of varying lengths

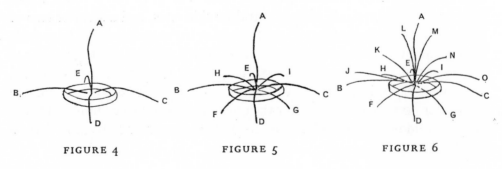

FIGURE 4   FIGURE 5   FIGURE 6

(J to O) are placed fan-like between B and C and, in a similar manner, a further six between D and E, thereby forming the basis of a rounded design. (Figure 6).

The shorter laterals are united together in the same way and the 'triangles' thus formed filled in with flowers and leaves to maintain the shape and hide the wire-netting.

In this type of arrangement it is specially important that every stem should appear to flow from the central axis, and even short-stemmed material should follow the main lines into the heart of the arrangement. Where colours are varied it is preferable that they should be concentrated in opposite 'triangles' rather than dotted about haphazardly.

Arrangements viewed from all sides: the oblong arrangement

This is one of the most popular shapes for dinner-table decorations as, being long and low, it does not obscure the view and yet it decorates adequately a considerable length of table. An oblong trough, vegetable dish or painted cake-tin are all suitable containers, but little will be seen of the actual vase in the final arrangement as the flowers should spill out on to the surface of the table. In view of the horizontal angles at which many of the stems must be inserted, it is advisable to use wire-netting over the top of the vase even if Florapak is the main method used to retain the stems.

The central stem (A) should not be so high as to become a barrier between persons sitting opposite each other. Twelve inches is about the maximum height for this particular stem. The long, lateral stems (B and C) can flow out at least one and a half times the length of the vase and some-

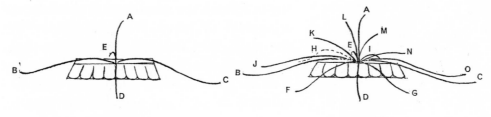

FIGURE 7   FIGURE 8

times very much longer. The short lateral stems (D and E) should be no more than the central stem and can be less, depending on the width of the table.

In general principle this style of arrangement is arranged in the same manner as the all-round arrangement, but the most important foliages and flowers should flow out as the long laterals and leaves and open flowers can suitably constitute the narrow side stems. (Figures 7 and 8.)

The cascading arrangement

This extremely graceful design can be arranged in any stemmed vase such as a goblet, a tall cake- or fruit-stand, a cherub holding a dish aloft or a dolphin balancing a bowl on its tail. These are all classical designs and can be found at sales, in junk shops or, quite probably, in your own china cupboard.

The final effect should be like a fountain, with emphasis on the central stems which should appear to carry the whole weight of the arrangement before letting it cascade over the sides. In this type of design the falling side stems are the longest and can be about one and a half times the total height of the vase, with the vertical and forward stems half this length. The vertical stem (A) should be inserted directly in line with the stem of the vase but should lean slightly backwards to balance the stems which will spill out in front. The lateral stems should fall steeply from the vase and, although stiff-stemmed flowers can be inserted at angles to give this effect, it is better to employ the curving stems of blossom or foliage which have in themselves lovely and desirable designs. The side stems (B and C) flow out from the same point as A but two more, (E and F), should be inserted behind these to flow at a backward angle, otherwise the arrangement will be unbalanced. (Figure 9.) Thereafter the filling-in follows the same steps as those for the triangular or fan-shaped arrangement, but the final effect should be particularly light and spontaneous, and should look, indeed, as if a bunch of flowers while held aloft had tumbled at will into a gentle and graceful design.

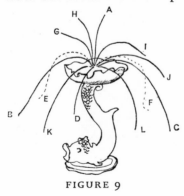

FIGURE 9

24

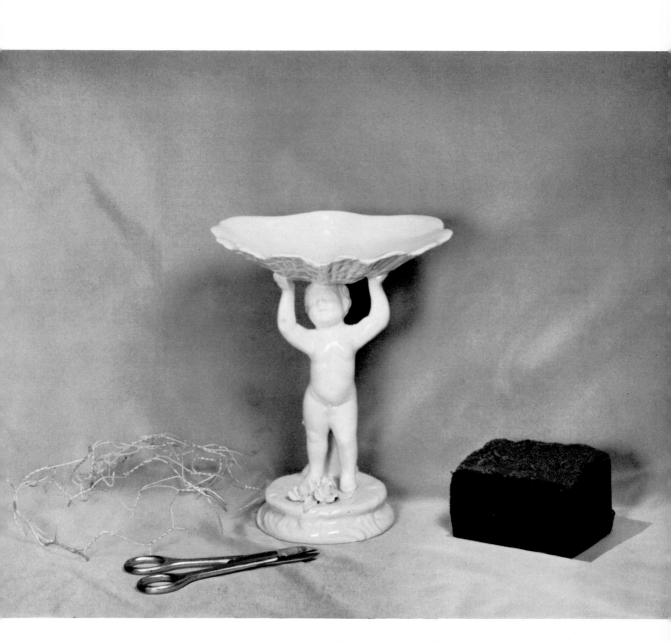

The problem of arranging flowers in very shallow containers has now been largely solved by Oasis which retains its shape when moistened so that flower stems can be inserted at all angles. Use only sufficient wire-netting to secure the block to the vase.

The two small illustrations show how a cascading design is first outlined with foliage and then filled in with flowers, all stemming
from a central point. The large illustration shows that even recessed
flowers follow the same lines into the heart of the arrangement.

Vases which have been used for the arrangements illustrated in this book. Their individual charm has added grace to the flowers they have contained.

MODERN DESIGNS

Many line arrangements seen today are, basically, adaptations of the delicately beautiful designs of Japanese flower decoration and, although this form of art is a study on its own, readers may be interested to know a little about its origins. Centuries ago Japanese flower arrangement was practised as a religious cult, and many of the original signs and symbols have been handed down through succeeding generations and are still in use. During the last thirty years various exponents of this art have taken it from its religious sphere and brought it into the world of today where its followers and students can be numbered in millions. Traditionally the lines of Japanese flower arrangement are based on a three-level approach in which the tallest stem or spray represents heaven, the medium one represents man, and the low one represents the earth, but the interpretations and intricacies involved can take years to absorb and understand. There is, however, much that can be learned from the Japanese appreciation of line which is fundamentally uncluttered and forceful.

A great deal of what is believed to be Japanese design is often the adaptation evolved in the United States, where the style became immensely popular as it required the minimum of flowers and was admirably suited to modern homes. In this country, perhaps because we possess a wealth of flowers which we are reluctant to ignore, we are apt to obscure the line by too much detail, with the result that flowers are forced into unnatural angles and the whole purpose of the clear surging lines of Japanese flower arrangement is lost.

The curved or L-shaped arrangement

This most elegant design is adaptable to many variations and suitable to many backgrounds. Although it can equally well be arranged in a trough with wire-netting and is most effective as a mantelpiece decoration, where the upright stem can follow the curve of a mirror, the following suggestions are given for an oblong dish with a central metal pin-holder.

This is essentially a design for blossom or foliage, as the long stems on which the line is based should simulate force and natural growth. The longest, slightly curving upright stem (A) can be up to twice the length of the dish, with the balancing horizontal stem (B) about three-quarters the

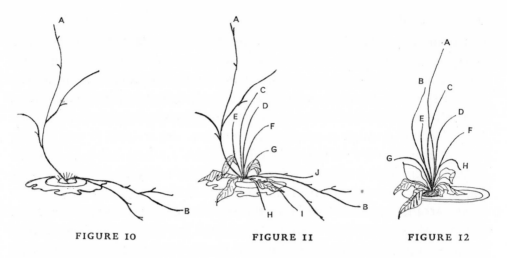

FIGURE 10   FIGURE 11   FIGURE 12

length of A. The upright stem is impaled firmly on the prongs of the pin-holder, and B is inserted at the same point and then bent into position and impaled horizontally. (Figure 10.) About five stems of flowers (C to G), preferably budded or pointed at the top, follow each other in diminishing lengths in line with A, the lower ones spreading out slightly from the base. Three stems of similar flowers, or leaves belonging to them (H to J), flow out in line with B, but the shortest should spill out towards the front to avoid a flat effect. (Figure 11.) Five largish leaves are now placed behind A, and at the side, in order to balance B. This is important, as otherwise, with no weight at the base, the arrangement could appear to be taking flight. If leaves are not available, short heavy pieces of blossom or foliage will serve the same purpose, but decapitated heads of tall flowers are better avoided as they cancel the natural effect.

The upright arrangement

This design is particularly suitable for the spiky, erectly growing flowers of spring. An oblong dish is required on which the pin-holder is placed at the side. If the dish is too shallow to hold water, the pin-holder can be put in a tin which can later be masked by moss or pebbles or by material similar to that used in the arrangement. The tallest, pointed stem (A) can be anything from the same, to one and a half times the length of the base, and should be impaled on the centre of the pin-holder. About seven or eight further pointed leaves or flowers are impaled at the same point and follow the line of the tallest stem in graduated lengths, three of the shorter ones spilling out a little from the base. (Figure 12.) Moss or pebbles will provide the necessary weight in a really fragile arrangement but, when heavier material is used, some of the leaves or foliage will be required for balance in the same manner as those used in the L-shaped arrangement.

A pillar arrangement in a cylindrical vase

This needs abrupt treatment as it is essentially a modern decoration. The effect is all the more dramatic if the axis is at the side, and a bare knotty branch, curved a little at its base, can provide the perfect start. (Figure 13.) Three or four large flowers can also be inserted perpendicularly one below the other, but if the branch should be of magnolias it is best left unadorned.

The single-stemmed arrangement

The bottle-necked vase has always been rather maligned but it has many uses if treated correctly. On a large scale it holds, and shows to perfection, a single branch of blossom or foliage, or an exotic lily stem. In miniature it can contain a rose or two, or some precious flower the beauty of which should stand alone. One and a half times the height of the vase is generally correct for any type of stem. (Figures 14 and 15.)

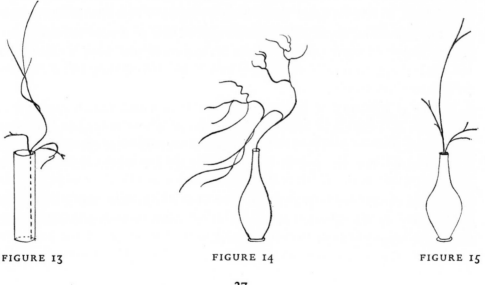

FIGURE 13   FIGURE 14   FIGURE 15

These are only a few of the designs devised to suit contemporary homes. They can be translated in a number of ways and are largely dependent on the eye of the arranger. A bare winter branch, a cascading fall of blossom, a knobbly stem of chestnut with the leaves bursting out of their green capsules, are all typical of the beauty which can be captured for our enjoyment if they are proportionately suitable to the vase and the background.

POINTS TO REMEMBER

1. Flower stems require cutting immediately prior to being placed in water. This applies to all flowers, whether they come from a shop or market, or have been recently gathered in a garden.

2. Stems should not be allowed to cross each other, as they would form thereby an impregnable barrier over the wire-netting and would also interrupt the flower lines desirable in most designs.

3. Certain stems, particularly woody ones, have nodules on them. These should be removed from the lower part of the stem, as otherwise they will get caught in the wire-netting and defy later removal should it become necessary.

4. Particular varieties of flowers should be so placed that they stem together in varying lengths from a joint base, thereby simulating natural growth and emphasizing their type and colour.

5. It is best to refrain from shortening stems until it is absolutely certain that this should be done. Even flowers placed low in a vase require a surprising length of stem and the whole arrangement will have a more light and natural appearance if no flowers look beheaded, as they can do if they are recessed too deeply.

6. Colour is best used in bold strokes, and it is worth remembering that white acts as a highlight and should be placed where emphasis is needed most. Dark flowers used centrally in a mixed arrangement can be beautiful at close range but are apt to disappear altogether when viewed from a distance.

7. Flowers should not be placed too near a fire or radiator, nor in a draught (which they dislike as much as we do). In all cases these conditions would curtail the length of their lives considerably.

Some hints on elementary floristry

I would be the last person to suggest that the exquisite art of floristry can be taught by the written word. It is essentially a skill which is learned by visual demonstration, and months, if not years, of practice are required before real proficiency can be attained. But, given that this fact is accepted, there are times when some knowledge of the wiring and mounting of flowers can prove extremely useful as, for instance, when Christmas decorations are being assembled or on those occasions when it is necessary to use mossed pads or rings instead of ordinary containers.

It should not, however, be imagined that even elementary floristry is easy. Few people realize quite how difficult it is until they hold a delicate flower in one hand and a wire in the other which will suddenly feel like a park railing, and after several broken heads and maltreated stems they may feel disinclined to persevere. All the same it is worth acquiring some dexterity in this aspect of flower arrangement as many more ideas can then be carried out and a diversity in styles of decorating is always welcome. Although it would be beyond the scope of this book to give more than a few general hints on this subject the following points may prove useful.

Some all-purpose wires will be necessary, those that are known as 22-gauge thickness by 12 inches long being the most useful. Florist's scissors

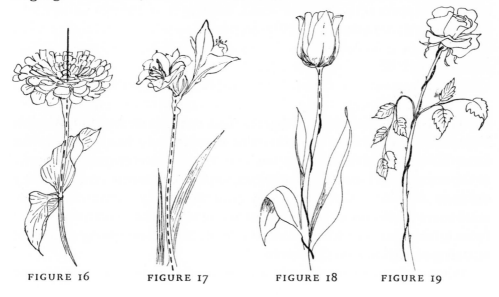

FIGURE 16   FIGURE 17   FIGURE 18   FIGURE 19

29

will also be required, as these cut wires as well as stems. Generally speaking there are two main methods of wiring flowers; firstly, the wiring of hollow-stemmed flowers where the wire is inserted inside the stem, and secondly, the wiring of solid-stemmed flowers where the wire is twisted around outside.

In the first case the procedure is as follows: hold the flower firmly in the left hand, and with the right hand push the wire straight through the centre of the flower and down the stem as far as it will go. This does no harm to the flower and has the advantage that the wire does not show. Alternatively, in stems that have flowerets rather than flower-heads, the wire should be inserted into the hollow stem from the base. The majority of flowers are, however, wired from the outside. Soft-stemmed flowers, such as tulips, are wired as follows: hold the stem as before in the left hand and insert the wire into the stem about an inch and a half below the flower and push it up into the flower-head, then wind the long remaining wire around the outside of the stem to the end.

For flowers that have hard stems, like roses or carnations, it is necessary to push the wire into the calyx and then wind it down the stem as unobtrusively as possible. Very few turns of the wire are required, and the stem should be held in the left hand and gently rotated while the wire is guided around the stem with the right hand, keeping it as straight as possible. These methods are illustrated in Figures 16–19.

Mounting flowers

When it is necessary to mount long-wired flowers, take the wired stem in the left hand and place a second wire crossways beneath it about an inch from the bottom, holding them together between the first finger and thumb. Now with the right hand bend the wire together like a hairpin and, in the same movement, wind the left prong over the right one enclosing the stem at the same time. Two complete twists, kept close together, are generally sufficient, but three may be necessary until proficiency is acquired as there must be no likelihood of the stems becoming loose. The two prongs should finish up the same length for insertion into the moss as one prong would not be strong enough to hold the flower.

When short-stemmed flowers are required it is possible to wire and

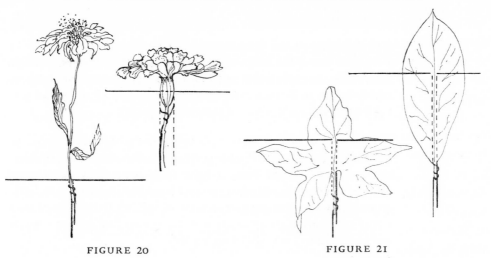

FIGURE 20   FIGURE 21

mount at the same time. An inch or two of natural stem should be left on the flower and the wire should be thrust horizontally through the calyx until the short end is two inches longer than the natural stem. Bend together like a hairpin and wind the long wire around the short one, enclosing the stem, so that two prongs of equal length are left for mounting. (Figure 20.)

Leaves may be required as well as flowers and the method with individual leaves is as follows: a fine stitch is taken with silver wire through the leaf from the back to contain the spine. The wire is then bent together, leaving a narrow loop down the back of the leaf, and the left prong is wound round the right prong to enclose a small piece of stem or the narrow base of the leaf. Thereafter it is mounted on the short wire stem in the same manner as for wired flowers. (Figure 21.)

Although I do not advocate the wiring of flowers for use in normal decoration there are occasions when it must be resorted to. Zinnias are an example, as unless they are wired through the head prior to being arranged the top-heavy flowers will bend over completely and thereby strangle themselves. Some very brittle, hollow-stemmed flowers, like amaryllis (Hippeastrum), can be strengthened, and even repaired when broken, by the insertion of a wire or two, or even a fine cane, into the base of the stem.

Wired and mounted flowers are necessary for the pads and rings described in the chapter on Church Decorations, and for the cones and rose trees described in Chapter 8.

31

A SILHOUETTE DESIGN

It is advantageous on occasions to place an arrangement in front of a window where the light coming from behind the flowers enhances their value. But it is important that the design is clean cut, with no untidy leaves to detract from the delicate tracery of stems and that the flowers themselves have a translucent quality.

In this arrangement of early forced lilac and eucalyptus foliage the window setting served a double purpose as mauve and purple flowers also generally benefit from a light from behind. In fact, casual though it may seem, this arrangement is entirely relative to its background as the pewter jug gives a sense of solidity to the base of such a semi-transparent group and repeats the tones of the leaded window and bare wistaria branches seen beyond.

It is particularly important that the long-stemmed leafless lilac illustrated here should be given a drink in deep water prior to arrangement and if, as sometimes happens, a head should droop despite this care the re-cutting and splitting of the stem with a renewal of the preliminary drink will generally bring the flower to life again.

Garden lilac looks more effective and lasts longer if partially de-foliated. Sprays of leaves can then be added where necessary.

ORCHIDS WITH EARLY SPRING FLOWERS
IN AN ORMOLU CANDELABRA

I use this elegant gilt and alabaster candelabra in a number of
different ways. It is, indeed, one of my favourite containers as the
delicacy of the ormolu compares favourably with even the most
fragile flowers. It is one of a pair which I was fortunate to find in
an antique shop in a remote part of Cornwall. Together they make
superb table decorations for important occasions, but there are
many times when I use them without candles for the beauty of the
stands alone which are a perfect foil for special flowers.

In this arrangement I have tried to repeat the delicate tracery of
the ormolu in the flowers above it and to suggest the clear tones of
early spring in a combination of shell pink, pale blue and golden
yellow. As I wanted to show every flower in the sprays of minute
golden oncidium orchids I used them on either side to indicate the
shape and followed the same lines with the pink-touched buds and
tiny flowers of *Jasminum polyanthum*. The small, lily-like, blue
flowers are *Leucocorynes ixioides odorato* (Glory of the Sun) which
originated in Chile but were not grown commercially in this country
until 1961. They are long-stemmed and long-lasting, and are a useful
adjunct at a time of year when other blue flowers are mostly short-
stemmed. A cluster of grape hyacinths (*Muscari*) repeated the blue
again, and solidity was added by the pale Lenten hellebores (which
had been given a long drink in warm water beforehand) and the
single pink camellia which was similar in tone to the candles and
the pattern on the Limoges china beneath it. Sprays of pink ivy-
leaved *Pelargonium peltatum* flow down in front and at either side.
This is a treasured possession in my greenhouse, as the lovely, waxy
leaves are invaluable for many bouquets as well as for decorative
trails among special flowers. In its natural state this plant is green
and white, but if kept in full sun the leaves will be touched with
pink as they are in the photograph. A few stems of sedum, and of
feathery *Pelargonium crispum* 'Variegatum', were added to supple-
ment the necessary green among the flowers, some of which had no
leaves of their own.

3. Backgrounds for Flowers

An interest in flower arrangement develops in people for a number of reasons, the chief of which is still, I believe, the decoration of their own homes. Nevertheless, the keen and competitive interest shared by all those who exhibit at the shows sponsored by the Royal Horticultural Society, and the National Association of Flower Arrangement Societies of Great Britain, indicates that flower arrangement has become of universal interest as well. Those of us who work with flowers as a profession are, perhaps, inclined to be over-dedicated people, but our interest now is tempered at most times by some apprehension, as our efforts are viewed by an increasingly knowledgeable and critical public.

Whatever the reason for our interest, the relationship between flowers and their setting is of paramount importance. The type of arrangement that is suitable for an individual room is not necessarily suitable for a public function; a line arrangement rarely has any place in a church, and the competitive arrangement, which must display every feature on the restricted space of a show bench, is not always the most satisfying decoration for a home. In fact, basically, the occasion and the background should determine the style of the decoration.

Decorations in private houses

In our homes the scope is endless; whatever the period of the house, or the style of its furnishings, backgrounds can generally be found to suit different designs in flower arrangement. A modern line decoration can be just as suitable in a sixteenth-century house as a more traditional one, nor is there any necessity to adhere too rigidly to modern arrangements just because our home is streamlined. It is where we put the flowers that matters.

We should try to avoid monotony by experimenting with new places for decoration, by finding different vases to suit seasonable arrangements, and by varying designs to emphasize the qualities of particular flowers. A change of position and style of decorating can be as refreshing to a room as a new set of curtains; after all, the whole purpose of flower arrangements in our home is surely a personal expression of beauty whereby we endeavour to enhance our surroundings by displaying flowers in the most attractive manner possible.

Arrangements for exhibitions

I think it should be accepted and understood that arrangements for exhibition purposes must adhere to rules in a manner that would not necessarily suit other circumstances. The space is restricted, and more often than not the design and type of material is decided by the organizers rather than the arranger. At other times a theme must be depicted where accessories are necessary in an already limited area. Because of these factors, and the limitations necessarily imposed by show-bench rules, arrangements at exhibitions do tend occasionally to become 'set pieces'. But this is not a matter for criticism; it is merely an example of the fact that flower arrangements must conform to the occasion, and that a type of arrangement which is suitable and beautiful in one place is not necessarily as good elsewhere. The proper blending of the flowers with their background, and the suitability of the style of decoration to the occasion, are the connecting links which can enable a well-arranged group to become, possibly, a superlative one.

Flowers in public places

Here the approach is rather different. Generally speaking the flowers have to last longer without, perhaps, the daily attention they would get in a private house. Whatever the design, the lines should be clear and firm and the flowers placed securely in the vase with every stem well below the water-level. An arrangement that might well appear solid and over-formal in a house would not be out of place in large surroundings. The impact of a well-designed firmly constructed group is far more telling under such conditions than a miscellaneous collection of small flowers, however beautiful they may be in themselves.

The importance of background

A suitable background is the backcloth for staging flower arrangements. White or very pale pastel-coloured walls display flowers in sharp relief and are unsurpassed for this purpose. Plain dark walls make an excellent foil for pale coloured flowers or, on occasions, for very striking bright ones such as all tones of clashing reds. Patterned walls, on the other hand, present difficulties, and flowers will show to better advantage if they are of one colour, either as emphasis to the predominating shade or in sharp contrast to it. In those places where the wall pattern is too ornate or, alternatively, the wall is heavily hung with pictures, it is advisable to move the flowers some distance away from the background so that they stand out on their own and the design of the arrangement is not confused with the fussiness behind it.

A window is an effective background for translucent flowers, or stems of blossom, where the light shining through the petals enhances their value. This is illustrated in the picture of lilac facing page 32. It is also advisable to place mauve or purple flowers in this position as they benefit from a light from behind, but it will detract from the solidity of an arrangement of massed flowers to place them against the light and double the amount of flowers may be necessary to achieve even quite a sparse effect. Mirrors, especially those that are beautifully framed, make an attractive background, but the design here should be clear-cut as the reflection can confuse an outline.

Lighting is very important. Where possible, flowers should be placed so that they are lit from the front at night, and where a light from above is available the effect of a spot-light can be obtained and flowers will assume a magical quality.

These are all fundamental points, but there are many others and, as one becomes increasingly observant, objects of interest and colour can be brought into prominence by the placing of relevant flower arrangements. The curtains may be an outstanding feature of a room and flowers can repeat and accentuate their colour, or a picture may dominate the scene and should be emphasized rather than disregarded. Good points are worth underlining and bad points are generally best ignored as an arrangement of flowers, however good, will not obliterate an eyesore and it is wiser to concentrate on a focal point of beauty rather than use flowers as a form of camouflage.

Salient positions for decorations

It is now, I think, a generally accepted fact that a few well-placed arrangements of a reasonable size are more effective than a number of small ones. Admittedly, as with all generalizations, there are many exceptions that leap to mind, such as the handful of special flowers on a desk, where they can be individually enjoyed, or, at midsummer, the desire to have just multitudes of roses everywhere. Nevertheless, the principle applies and should certainly be considered where decorations for parties are concerned. Although there can be no hard-and-fast rules about suitable positions for flowers, as these must depend on the shape of the room, the furniture, the lighting and, of course, the occasion, it is worth remembering that levels should be different. If a tall arrangement is placed on a pedestal or mantelpiece it needs to be balanced by another of preferably different shape at table level. Arrangements should also be distributed on both sides of a room to avoid the effect of a row of flowers. And if the furnishings and the occasion permit, a single, central arrangement can be very lovely indeed.

On the whole, flowers placed opposite the entrance of a room make the greatest impact on entering it. An entrance hall is generally a good place for a flower arrangement (provided it is kept out of a draught), and an all-round arrangement at the foot of a curving staircase is most effective as it can be regarded from above as well. Decorations are generally best kept to the table in a dining-room, as this is often the only place lit at night. It is also, in most cases, the main feature of the room. Decorations for parties or public functions are best kept high, most of them at shoulder level, as it should be possible to see the flowers when people are standing up. This also, of course, applies to decorations in churches.

One position where I have never cared to see flowers is in a fireplace. This may be a personal prejudice as it is quite usual to see a hearth filled with flowers or plants, especially in summer, but in my defence I feel flowers dislike it too, as it is inevitably draughty and can also be dirty, causing the flowers to become soot-spotted. Even if both these disadvantages are overcome it still serves very little useful purpose, as an ugly fireplace cannot be hidden by such decorations and a good one is a feature of beauty in itself.

Colour

A sense of colour is rather like an ear for music; you either possess it or you do not. Colour also appeals to different people in different ways, and it would be unwise and indeed presumptuous to lay down any hard-and-fast rules about it. There are, however, some established methods which help towards the achievement of certain desired effects in flower arrangement, as it is important that flowers should maintain their colour form when cut, in much the same manner as they do in natural growth. An arrangement consisting of different types of flowers of the same colour requires an infinite variety in the shades of the tone concerned, as otherwise a curiously flat effect will result. If a full-blown rose is studied carefully it is apparent that a multitude of harmonizing shades are contained within it, from the brightest inside petals to the paling outside ones. Similarly an entirely red group of flowers would have little impact if it were all of one tone. It should go through the whole gamut of reds, from pink to crimson, and the more brilliant and different the variations the more effective it will be. The same principle applies to other colours, pale or dark.

It is often said that flowers never clash in colour as man-made things can do. This is true enough while flowers are growing, as the varied greens and greys of adjacent foliage, and the different depths of shade provided by the flowers in bud and those in full bloom, add the softness which brings harmony to the whole picture. Inevitably when cut flowers are arranged indoors they are moved from their natural environment into an artificial one, and we should endeavour to provide the complementary differences in shade which they possess in growth.

The colours of many specific types of flowers will blend when arranged together. Annuals such as stocks, shirley poppies or zinnias, despite their immense range of colour, are cases in point. It is only when hybridization interferes too much with natural tones that we need to be selective.

Certain exceptionally strong colours, such as orange, flame or scarlet, require a cool tone to moderate them. Most shades of green will have the desired effect, and among the richer tones of autumn, copper and bronze and sepia shades will add the necessary moderation. The subtle, rather obscure shades of lavender, orchid mauves, purple and maroon can be unbelievably beautiful in daylight, but must be exceptionally well-lit if they are to retain their beauty at night. They are wasted against a dark background or in a dim corner. Many of the darker and softer shades of blue also lose their colour in artificial light, but the pale tones, particularly turquoise blue, are effective at most times.

In arrangements of mixed colours it is important that the different colours are carried in drifts rather than dotted about spasmodically. Many arrangements of this type require a central high-light, and white will provide this in groups of pastel colours, shades of silvery pinks, lemon yellows or in any of the subtle mauve tones. White is, however, too sharp a contrast to introduce suddenly among many bright flowers, or even among dark ones, and it is better to use cream, or very pale tones of the predominating colour, to get the required effect. On the whole it is generally advisable to use light-coloured flowers for the outline and centre of an arrangement and to tuck the darker ones in low to provide depth, but care must be taken when such groups are used for public functions. Dark flowers can disappear altogether when viewed from a distance, so it is important that all those that constitute the shape, both in outline and depth, are provided by paler varieties of flowers.

The blending of colour, or colour contrast, is essentially a personal affair because something that can be wholly satisfying to one person can be the reverse to someone else. Prejudices can be overcome all the same. An arrangement of flowers is, of necessity, only a transient affair, and we lose little by experimenting with colours outside our usual range, while we stand to gain a great deal in a wider field of pleasure. In fact, such experimentation can be one of the most rewarding and exciting aspects of the whole fascinating pursuit of flower arrangement.

Vases

Vases are quite as important as the flowers we put in them. Almost anything that pleases the eye can be used as a vase. Tin linings can be made to fit those not intended originally to hold water, or we can substitute with cake-tins or more adaptable plastic bowls.

It is impossible to generalize about vases except to say that they should be in accord with personal taste and suitable to their background, blending with the furniture, the décor and the flowers to be used. Just as a classical urn would seem out of place in a modern kitchen-cum-dining-room, so would a copper jug or striped jar be alien to a gracious drawing-room or dignified church.

There are some designs which are almost basic necessities in the vase cupboard of any arranger of flowers. First of all I think I would put the wide-lipped classical bowl on a short stem and firm base which is similar to many antique lead garden urns. This is suitable for a variety of different arrangements and allows ample room for the placing of a number of horizontal stems. I would put next in importance the goblet-shaped vase, or any vase on a tall stem which permits the graceful down-flowing lines of a cascading arrangement. It can be used equally well for massed cones or domes of flowers, as the long stem mitigates against a squat effect. The completely classical urn is necessary for many formal arrangements such as church groups, but for ordinary purposes I think a less formal shape is preferable. Some round or oblong bowls, deep and shallow rectangular troughs, a few flat dishes and possibly a straight cylindrical vase are further essential requirements for the vase cupboard. 'Little' vases can be almost anything that is available, such as wine glasses, shells, china boxes or tiny baskets.

When vase hunting it is worth remembering that it is the shape and not the value that is of importance; many lovely objects can be found at sales or in junk shops which, though low in price due to chips or cracks, are still most desirable as vases, as flowers can hide their imperfections. Consider the choice available: china and pottery (both antique and modern), alabaster, crystal, mother-of-pearl, glass, old silver, pewter, bronze, copper, wrought iron, wood and basket-work all have their place in the vase cupboard, awaiting, with the seasons and occasions, their rightful place in the scheme of flower arrangement. The illustration facing page 25 shows a number of vases which have been used for arrangements throughout the book. It is apparent, I think, that all possess some charm and thereby lend added grace to the flowers which later they contain.

Every year the designs of modern pottery improve; vases are designed to suit all styles of decoration from perfect copies of classical urns and chalices to the most streamlined shapes for simple line arrangements. There should be no necessity for novelty. Teapots and kettles have spouts for other uses than the emergence of flowers, and household utensils are made for utilitarian purposes and few add to the adornment of our homes.

SOME PRACTICAL FLOWER ARRANGEMENTS

The following suggestions for arrangements of familiar flowers against various backgrounds are based on ideas and sketches contained in this chapter and the previous one. They are mainly elementary but are offered as a guide to the inexperienced in the hope that they may prove useful as a starting-point for individual experiments in all fields of flower arrangement.

An L-shaped arrangement of yellow spring flowers

Flowers required: Two stems of forsythia. One bunch of either daffodils or yellow irises. A few wild arum leaves or, alternatively, a few fern fronds cut from a house plant.

Recommended vase: A shallow oval dish in either white, pale grey or celadon green, or an oblong tin covered with silvery bark.

The two stems of forsythia, slightly curved if possible, form the angle as shown in Figure 10, page 26. Within it the daffodils or irises should follow the same lines and the wild arum leaves, or fern fronds, should be inserted at the base to provide balance and weight. Yellow flowers are particularly good against a pale green background or one of dark oak panelling.

It is worth remembering that a more natural effect is achieved if material that normally grows close to the ground is placed at the base of these line arrangements.

An upright arrangement of spring flowers in shades of blue

Flowers required: Three straight stems of silvery palm. A bunch of blue irises. Three *Begonia rex* leaves, cut from a plant and given a drink beforehand.

41

Recommended vase: An oval dish or long narrow trough in pale pink or grey glazed pottery.

The palm, together with about five irises, is impaled on a pinholder in descending lengths as shown in Figure 12, page 26. As weight is required at the base for flowers of this size it can be indicated by the leaves of *Begonia rex.* These soft tones would look well against a window, in front of a mirror or with a pinkish-grey background.

A pink triangular arrangement of early summer flowers

Flowers required: About five stems of Whitebeam, partly in bud. Seven stems of shell-pink gladioli, preferably the primulinus variety. A bunch of pale pink stock. Seven pink peonies. A few sprays of pink garden roses. A bunch of long-stemmed pink sweet peas. Either three grey hosta leaves or short sprays of Whitebeam.

Recommended vase: A wide-lipped classical bowl or urn in either shell-pink, grey or old silver.

The Whitebeam should form the outline and be inserted as A, B and C and also as I and J in Figure 1, page 20. A stem of gladiolus is now placed immediately in front of A to form the tallest point, and two more follow the lines of B and C to bring colour to the outline. The hosta leaves, or sprays of foliage, are placed at right angles to A and should spill downwards over the rim of the vase. The filling-in starts with four more stems of gladioli being inserted on either side of A, as E to H, and then the stock should follow the lines of I and J and also be inserted as K and L. All the stems which have been inserted so far should appear to stem from the same central point or to flow sideways, in line with each other, from the heart of the arrangement. The peonies are now inserted between A and D to form a swelling curve, some of them being recessed quite low in the vase for depth, and the sprays of garden roses should flow forward on one side and be balanced on the other by a drift of long-stemmed sweet peas. Any gaps which are left between the outline and the central curves can be filled in by the shorter stems of stock and, towards the centre, full-blown garden roses will provide the necessary additional depth both in apparent weight of flower and colour. The arrangement should now be viewed from the side

42

and, where necessary, additional pieces of foliage should be inserted at a slightly backward angle behind A to provide balance. Silvery-pink flowers are good against all pastel-coloured backgrounds but are lost against those of cream or gold. They are also beautiful with lime green or clear lemon yellow, but pale grey panelling, or grey stone, are perhaps the most satisfactory backgrounds of all.

A mid-summer all-round arrangement of mixed white flowers

Flowers required: A bunch of long-stemmed white sweet peas. A dozen stems of herbaceus white campanulas or side shoots of white delphiniums. A dozen small white roses, such as those which could be cut from sprays of the perfect floribunda 'Iceberg'. A bunch of white dianthus (pinks). A few trails of variegated ivy.
Recommended vase: Any round bowl in a pastel shade, or a fruit dish of glass or silver.

This all-round arrangement should, in effect, slightly resemble an opened umbrella when finished. A stem of campanula, or small delphiniums, should be inserted as A and the remainder placed horizontally for all eight laterals as shown in Figures 4 and 5, page 22, with trails of the ivy placed between them to soften the lines. The sweet peas can now be inserted in groups as J to O between B and C and in a similar manner between D and E, thereby forming the design. (Figure 6.) The roses and pinks are used to join the shorter laterals to A and also to give weight and depth to the arrangement. If the bowl is very shallow it is sometimes necessary to place a metal pin-holder under the wire-netting to hold the central stems firmly in place or, alternatively, a block of dampened Oasis can be used instead if suitably tethered to the container by wire-netting.

White flowers are effective against most backgrounds, including white. The arrangement described here would make a good table centre, particularly on a table of dark polished wood.

A cascading arrangement of late summer flowers in shades of lavender and mauve

Flowers required: Seven stems of grey foliage, such as *Senecio laxifolius*. About seven trails of clematis or *Cobaea scandens*. A few stems of maroon-coloured alliums or purple phlox. A dozen mauve roses, such as 'Prelude' or 'Sterling Silver'. A dozen lavender carnations.

Recommended vase: A silver lustre dolphin or tazza-shaped vase in china or alabaster.

Long stems of the grey foliage are inserted horizontally to form all the down-flowing laterals as shown in Figure 9, page 24. A shorter one of about half their length is inserted directly in line with the stem of the vase but should tilt slightly backwards for balance. The trails of clematis or *Cobaea scandens* should follow the lines of the foliage, but one, at least, should spill forwards towards the stem of the vase in a gentle curve. A drift of three roses, preferably on budded stems, now placed at right angles to the shorter, central pieces of foliage and should flow forwards and downwards for the same length. Another rose is placed directly in front of the foliage and four more are inserted at angles to form a swelling curve between this and those roses which spill forwards. The remaining roses are then placed on either side of, and slightly behind, the curve to indicate depth. The carnations can then be inserted in varying lengths on both sides to complete the outline down the long laterals. Further carnations follow the same lines into the heart of the arrangement, and it is important that some lines should flow backwards as well as forwards, as otherwise the group will look unbalanced. These steps are illustrated in Figure 9, page 24. The alliums or phlox, which are the darkest flowers among these quiet colours, should be placed fairly low in the vase, on either side of the roses, to add apparent weight. They should not, however, be recessed too deeply, as a light and spontaneous effect is only achieved by keeping stems as long as possible, compatible with the desired design. These muted, shadowy tones have a richness, nevertheless, and would be beautiful against a soft grey-green background or one of grey alone.

An oblong arrangement of autumn flowers in shades of apricot and flame

Flowers required: Six trails of small vine leaves and five stems of peony foliage, both reddened with autumn tints. A few sprays of berberis with coral berries. Nine stems of montbretia. A dozen flame or orange roses such as 'Katharine Petchold'. A dozen small apricot-coloured dahlias. A few cream zinnias.

44

Recommended vase: An oblong trough in copper or bronze, or a long cake-tin painted cream.

The peony foliage should be used for the central stem and for the shorter laterals, while the trails of vine leaves could form the long laterals B and C and also the slightly shorter ones as shown in Figures 7 and 8, page 23. The montbretia, in groups of three in varying lengths, should follow the long laterals and also be inserted as a central spray, a shade higher than the peony foliage. The roses can now follow the lines of the longest stems B and C and also across to D and E thereby uniting the central stem with the four points. The berries should be placed near the centre to indicate weight, and the open-faced dahlias and zinnias should complete the filling-in, but flow through to 'triangles' opposite to each other. These autumn-tinted flowers look well against a cream or sepia background or where there are comparable colours in the furnishings.

A pillar arrangement for winter in brown and bronze

Flowers required: A bare, knotty branch of suitable shape (walnut is tough and grows in unusual forms). Three bronze chrysanthemums.

Recommended vase: A tubular design of Scandinavian pottery in cinnamon brown.

The branch should be placed at the right of the vase and it may be necessary to prune it a little to the desired shape as shown in Figure 13, page 27. If the branch is heavy it is sometimes advisable to wedge it in place rather than use wire-netting, and this can be done with four small pieces of wood as shown in Figure 31, page 117. The three chrysanthemums should follow the main stem of the branch, one below the other, starting about a third of the way from the top. These varied browns would be effective against a dark green, dull gold or ivory background. Also, as the line is definite, the arrangement should stand out against a patterned wall.

The single-stemmed vase

Although the bottle-necked vase can display a single branch of blossom to perfection, it is perhaps more useful on a smaller scale when it holds the last of the autumn roses or the very first spring flowers, such as *Helleborus niger* or *Iris unguicularis* (better known, perhaps, as *I. stylosa*). There are many modern designs, both in pottery and glass, which are suitable for this purpose, but most china cupboards can produce something which will serve as well, from the discarded ginger jar to the miniature scent bottle. On a large scale, one branch is generally sufficient, as shown in Figure 14, page 27, and it is particularly effective with almond blossom or Japanese quince (now called chaenomeles). On a small scale, up to three flowers can be displayed as in Figure 15, page 27, but, to avoid overcrowding these slender vases, it is preferable to use buds with one open flower or, as in the case of the lovely budded stems of the white Christmas rose (*Helleborus niger*), one stem alone would be sufficient.

Flowers on their own

There is a slight trend at the moment to make flower decorations so natural and simple that no aids to arrangement are used at all. This may well be a natural swing of the pendulum away from the over-arranged or too stylized decoration of recent years, but such a seemingly artless effect nevertheless requires a certain skill. In complete contradiction to all normal rules, stems should be allowed to cross each other and form thereby a 'netting' of their own. A vase shaped like a goldfish bowl, or a tub, is the most suitable, and flowers should be placed round the sides first with the stems meeting towards the middle. This method is continued until the vase is almost full, and the flowers are, in effect, lying in graduated layers. The final flowers are placed upright in the centre to complete what will have become a mound of flowers, and the interlocking stems will hold the vertical ones firmly in place.

4. Spring Flowers and Blossom

More than at any other time of the year, I think, there are flowers to suit every individual taste in the flood of colour that breaks upon the world during the spring. The fact that it is all so transient and dependent upon our unpredictable climate, when an untimely frost may blacken overnight something that was clothed in beauty the day before, makes us, perhaps, all the more eager to re-create in our homes a semblance of the loveliness that can be so short-lived outside. As with all flower arrangements a lightness of touch, and an emphasis on the natural habits and individuality of the flowers concerned, is particularly important at this time. Any appearance of over-arrangement is best avoided, as there is such spontaneity in all growing things in spring that we should try to capture the effect of a gay, fleeting beauty with all the dexterity at our command. Blossom should retain its fragility; little flowers are best used in sufficient quantity to maintain their colour and yet not lose their essential airiness of growth; and great regard should be given to the particular personalities of the abundant, but often strong-willed, flowers of spring.

Before we start gathering and arranging the flowers, however, it is worth considering the best vantage points on which to put them, the most suitable backgrounds for the type of groups we envisage and the vases most in keeping with the season's flowers. Inevitably requirements change with the time of year, and the more we use variety in all concepts of flower arranging the more creative we become. Because everything is new and fresh at this time of year, I think the emphasis should be on simplicity. A pale, or really dark background is generally best, although such flowers as daffodils and bluebells, and many forms of blossom, show to best advantage in front of a window.

FREESIAS FROM A CORNISH FLOWER FARM

Although freesias have become such popular winter-flowering green-house plants that they now appear in the shops from autumn onwards, they still remain in essence forerunners of spring. Their strongly-fragrant, many-coloured flowers will always be for me an indication of future profusion as they come at a time when we are so circumscribed by winter's short chill days.

I wonder, however, if people who derive pleasure from out-of-season flowers realize at all the efforts that go into their production? The golden yellow freesias shown here came from Derek Tangye's flower farm at Minack; those of you who have read his books about his life there will appreciate how many of these early flowers are the result of endless struggles with unpredictable weather conditions which can at times despoil the perfection of greenhouse plants just as much as those that have no protection from the changing skies.

The effects of fog, prolonged frosts or unseasonable heat waves can dictate success or failure regardless of careful planning. Fog will infiltrate a greenhouse to blear the perfection of the flowers within. Prolonged frosts are not only killers to outside plants but increase the price of packing, as flowers must be adequately insulated against the cold. And too early a spring will upset the balance between indoor and outdoor flowers so that both reach maturity together.

Such flowers, then, as freesias, early daffodils, irises and anemones are the product of the grower's constant gamble with nature when high hopes and disappointments alternate. The same applies, of course, to all things growing, but never more so than when flowers are forced into growth ahead of their natural season.

THE FIRST DAFFODILS AND DOUBLE TULIPS

Despite their loveliness daffodils and tulips are not the easiest flowers to arrange. This photograph was taken in February when daffodils are often sold without any accompanying leaves and the first double tulips have a fragile air.

It is a wise extravagance at this time of year to buy some long-lasting foliage which will provide a background for several different varieties of early spring flowers. Here, in a very simple white mantle vase, I have arranged three stems of *Elaeagnus pungens* 'Maculata' as the gleaming golden yellow on the patterned leaves is identical with the gold of daffodils and, in this case, of the tulips too. This is one of the most useful and effective winter evergreens as it has the advantage of lasting for weeks in water if the vase is kept well replenished.

It can be seen that the axis of the arrangement is slightly off centre as I wished to follow the sloping line of the oak beam and also to display the long stems of the brilliant foliage. All flowers and leaves flow out from the same point which is, I think, of paramount importance where spring flowers are concerned as these grow naturally in clumps together. The rather stiff daffodils follow the upright stem while the more malleable tulips follow all three lines of foliage and are also placed centrally to give the necessary appearance of weight. Later in the spring similar arrangements could be made with a background of hazel catkins or willow palm from the hedgerows.

The white varieties of trumpet daffodils are becoming increasingly popular and have great charm in decoration. They look best, I think, among flowers which have the same purity of tone and I like to use them with pale, pastel-coloured hyacinths and any of the early flowering almonds or cherries.

There are many objects we can use as vases for spring flowers which would not necessarily be suitable at other times of the year. Baskets, in all shapes and sizes, are particularly good. So also are wooden salad or bread bowls and flat pottery vegetable dishes, as they have a country look about them eminently suitable for the simpler flowers. Glass or crystal vases, which are not normally easy to use because they show the often untidy stems of flowers, can now be used successfully. If the wire is fitted over the top of the vase, instead of inside, the stems of such flowers as daffodils, bluebells, freesias and hyacinths, which are clean of leaves, can look as lovely through the glass as the flowers above them. There is a vast variety of wine goblets, fruit dishes, witch bowls and coloured glass cornucopias which lend themselves to such arrangements. Old silver sweet dishes, bread baskets or boxes (with the lids propped open), together with pewter jugs or tankards, make a perfect setting for all pastel-coloured arrangements. And any pieces of mother-of-pearl are real treasures, as they seem to catch and reflect the pale translucence of the early flowers in a manner undreamed of until you have tried it yourself. A metal holder, available in most good flower shops, inserted into the top of any pretty candlestick immediately transforms it into a perfect vase for small mixed arrangements. And for single, glorious branches of blossom which are capable of forming a line arrangement on their own, one can use a tall, slender vase, or that lovely jar with the narrow neck hitherto considered so useless for other flowers. Indeed, the scope is endless and the search among forgotten pieces can be greatly rewarding. Sometimes, perhaps for the sake of being 'different', I have seen objects used as vases which were both unattractive and out of place. The whole purpose of flowers is surely to be beautiful and to give pleasure, and in our efforts to attain this in our homes we should avoid any appearance of 'stunting'. Let us say that any object is suitable provided it helps to enhance the natural beauty of the flowers and is in keeping with the place we wish to decorate.

The early flowers of spring
My personal inclination is to arrange early spring flowers in great simplicity, mainly by themselves, in an effort to retain their initial delicacy.

Snowdrops, the little hardy cyclamens with absurdly ornate leaves, violets, crocuses and primroses are all so fragile individually that only by gathering a handful, and retaining them together, is it possible to catch the effect they give while growing. They can be arranged on their own in any suitable small vase or basket, and it is often best to leave those already bunched in the shop intact with the string around them. A shallow bowl filled entirely with closely bunched violets or primroses is an enchanting sight and, on the same principle, a variety of small flowers can be arranged together to simulate a carpet of growing flowers. For this type of arrangement a flat vegetable dish which has been rather sparsely filled with crumpled wire-netting is most suitable. Various varieties of small flowers, with their own leaves, are inserted in bunches through the netting and can differ as you like in height and colour. Space can be left between the little groups and the intervening gaps covered in moss, to give the effect of a miniature garden.

Christmas and Lenten roses

These flowers have a unique quality of beauty, perhaps because some appear while winter is still with us, and because all varieties have delicate chalice-shaped flowers on budded stems unlike so many of the early spring flowers which are spiky. The white Christmas rose (*Helleborus niger*), despite its looks to the contrary, is of fairly tough calibre and lasts well when cut, but the later Lenten roses need more attention. Even after initial treatment in hot water it is often necessary to remove them to a cool room at night, as they dislike too warm an atmosphere, but if, despite this care, they still tend to droop, refreshment in deep water will generally revive them. To my mind they are well worth the trouble, as they lend themselves to many subtle combinations of colours and range from ivory, tinged with dark green and occasionally speckled like a bird's egg, through dusky pinks, mauves and purples, to perhaps the loveliest of all, the sea-green of the Corsican hellebore. A handful of *Helleborus orientalis*, ranging in colour from greenish-white to plum, were used as the main feature in the little group facing page 17. They were arranged in a miniature grey alabaster urn, the mottled shadings of which toned with the quiet colours of the flowers, and their companions were a few pieces from the greenhouse. The pinkish buds of *Jasminum polyanthum* blended with the pale hellebores, as did the ivy-leaved *Pelargonium peltatum*, while the feathery green and white *Pelargonium crispum* 'Variegatum' and silver *Senecio leucostachys* added lightness to what might have been too sombre an arrangement. Only the plum-coloured hellebores wilted under the hot lights of photography and required replacement. The remainder not only survived the session but remained fresh for several days thereafter.

Freesias and anemones

One rarely sees freesias in sufficient quantity as they are a comparatively expensive flower to buy and, to my mind, one requires a great number to get any effect of shape and colour. They are, I think, definitely best on their own, arranged in a tumbling design in a tall stemmed glass goblet or fruit dish where the delicate stems can droop at will. In the illustration facing page 48 at least three bunches of yellow freesias were used as, in order to get an effect of colour, a number of stems had to be inserted in varying lengths so that the flower-heads followed each other back into the heart of the arrangement. Anemones, on the other hand, are cheap and one may indulge in a large quantity with a free conscience. The paler types mix well with other flowers, but the brilliant red, puce and purple varieties are best left to display their brilliance together. I like to arrange them in a dark vase in order to emphasize their black centres.

Daffodils

Daffodils are to many the epitome of spring and, in their infinite variety, are in such profusion that every house contains them. Perhaps because of this, justice is not always done in the matter of arrangement. They are to me essentially upright flowers, assuming few natural curves of their own, and I like to see them rising together from a central base. In mixed arrangements I think they should stem from one place rather than be used as an outline or be haphazardly intermingled with other flowers. They are perhaps at their best either alone with their own buds and leaves or in combination with delicate branches of spring foliage or blossom such as pale green catkins, palm, cornelian cherry or forsythia. Daffodils lend themselves well to a simple line arrangement, but, as always with such groups, the material should look as if it was following its natural habit of growth and not as if it had been forced into an alien line.

The illustration between pages 56 and 57 shows a few orange-centred narcissi named 'Glorification' arranged within the curve of two stems of budding Horse Chestnut. The stones were added to balance the weight of the heavy branches and from between them rose the delicate fronds of a house plant fern.

Tulips

With daffodils, tulips are to every flower-minded person such an essential feature of the spring scene that no chapter on this subject could omit them. Their variety is numberless and their range of colour becomes such a bewildering kaleidoscope of shining brilliance that it is impossible to attempt description. Nor could any suggestions given here be remotely comprehensive or remain, even for a season, up to date, but a few words on the flowers themselves may be helpful. It is not always remembered that tulips have a determined will of their own and grow their own way in water regardless of the wishes of the arranger. This fact presents a problem when incorporating them in a mixed arrangement, and they are better used in a more casual manner where the lovely lines they develop do not throw out a planned design. It is best to start with them straight, however, and they require several hours in deep water, closely wrapped in paper and with every stem re-cut, before any attempt is made to use them.

Tulips retain their shape best in a mixed arrangement if placed in a sweeping line with the stems following each other in varying lengths. Even if the heads now curl upwards the line of colour remains intact and the plan of the arrangement is not affected. It is helpful sometimes to turn back the petals of a few single tulips, thereby transforming the flower into an open-faced one. If this is done with gentleness no damage occurs, and it has the advantage of emphasizing the colour and adding variety to the design. The peony-flowered tulips are valuable in larger and more formal groups. They retain the initial position in which they have been placed better than the other varieties, perhaps because their heads are heavier and less easy to lift towards the light. The glorious white 'Mount Tacoma', shell-pink 'Eros' and 'Lilac Perfection' are excellent examples and well worth growing in any garden.

Facing page 49 is a group combining daffodils with early double tulips and evergreen variegated elaeagnus which was arranged in a simple, oblong mantle vase. Although the background here was a white wall, interlaced with dark oak beams, this type of arrangement would be equally suitable in a modern room as the lines are clear-cut. Three stems of elaeagnus were inserted to form the outlines, one of which followed the rather dramatic line of the oak beam. The daffodils rose from a central source to follow the main stem, while the tulips added solidity and were placed to droop down in front to give the necessary appearance of weight.

In the hope that they may be helpful in suggesting other combinations of colour and design the following are a few well-remembered arrangements incorporating various types of tulips:

1. Many of the slender, pointed lily-flowered tulips are very suitable for table decorations and I have used 'China Pink' or 'White Duchess' to great effect in either a mother-of-pearl or porcelain shell, letting them trail from it on to the polished surface of the table in the manner of convolvulus.

2. The scarlet, cream-edged 'Aladdin' and violet 'May Time' are dramatic flowers that look well in rather a stark arrangement against an outline of lichen-covered or magnolia-budded branches.

3. Any pink varieties of tulip are particularly beautiful if arranged in old silver or pewter, the soft sheen of which will reflect the silvery tones of the flowers. The double rose-tinged 'Murillo', arranged with pink lilac and pink japonica (*Chaenomeles speciosa* 'Moerloosei') or early *Prunus cerasifera* 'Nigra' (formerly called *P. pissardii*), the almost silver 'Pink Admiration', with equally pale palm branches, and leaves of silver *Begonia rex* are typical examples.

4. Exciting and unusual arrangements can be made with any of the new green Viridiflora tulips, or with some of the lovely, serrated-edged Parrot tulips, many of which are streaked with green. Arranged with wild arums and their triangular leaves, the outline softened with the green heads of early guelder rose, these quiet tones can be most arresting.

5. Against some backgrounds, notably silver grey panelling, the more sombre and subtle-hued tulips can contribute to memorable arrangements. Of these the Bybloems, Bizarres and Rembrandts provide the most striking

selections, being reminiscent of tulips pictured in Dutch and Flemish flower paintings. Indeed the list is endless, and memory begets memory, because among no other variety of spring flowers is the selection of colour, shape and type so varied.

Irises

Irises are not the easiest flowers to arrange. Like daffodils, they are upright in growth and need, I think, to stem from a central source, It is generally advisable to place a few stems of variegated lengths one in front of the other, as the open flowers die quickly and sufficient buds should be available to take their place. Between pages 72 and 73 is an illustration of a vertical arrangement of blue irises and palm stems rising from a base of *Begonia rex* leaves. Provided they are given a good drink initially these seemingly soft-textured leaves will last a long time when cut even when, as in this arrangement, they were impaled on a pin-holder in comparatively shallow water.

Blossom

How often have we gazed, almost in awe, at the sudden white cloud of blossom that can appear, practically overnight, in early spring? Surely everyone has wished, as I have done, to capture this effect in a decoration, but what was ethereal outside can too often become rather heavy, over-leaved branches indoors. The nearest I have come to achievement is with philadelphus, and if I describe it here I am almost out of this chapter and into that of 'Summer Abundance'; but it is relative in that it, perhaps more than any other blossom, can call to mind a cloud when arranged indoors. Branches of varying lengths and shapes, stripped largely of their leaves and arranged in a willow tree design where the light falls on them, make a decoration that is so simple, yet so lavishly flowered and so fragrantly scented, that the effect is magical. Of course, it takes time and I cannot say it lasts overlong, but if the stems are picked while many of the flowers are still in bud it will retain its quite breathtaking beauty for several days. The same principle applies to garden lilac, which lasts better and is more effective as a decoration if most of the heavy leaves are removed beforehand. In both cases a great number of stems are required in order to achieve an effect of blossom in growth, as the branches dwindle considerably when

55

the leaves are removed. The leafless lilac, which appears in the shops in early spring, is generally best used in conjunction with other flowers and foliage as it is apt to be rather stiff and top-heavy if arranged on its own. In the illustration between pages 56 and 57, pale mauve, leafless lilac is shown arranged with grey eucalyptus foliage in an antique silver water-jug which provided depth for the long stems and also had a lip wide enough to permit the casual spilling-out effect of a tree in bloom.

On the other hand, a single branch of some of the spring blossoms can be sufficient decoration by itself. Personally, although I will prune branches to suit my requirements of size and shape, I am against forcing them into curves and angles they do not bear naturally, and prefer to use them in such places where their own design would seem suitable. It is often possible to let a stem follow the lines of an arched door or window, or the curve of a mirror. Indeed, any salient features in a room can be brought into prominence by the emphasis of a suitably placed, and beautifully shaped, branch of blossom. This point is illustrated facing page 72 where two stems of flowering crab-apple (*Malus hupehensis*) curve round a mirror while azaleas and globular heads of *Viburnum plicatum tomentosum* give body to the centre of this L-shaped arrangement.

Camellias

Both for its foliage and its flowers the camellia is one of the richest assets of this time of year. I have an old tree in my garden which in early spring is completely covered in deep pink double flowers. The tree itself falls in such a graceful rounded shape, with cascades of flowers almost reaching to the ground, that it is a subject for a decorator's contemplation. Although the foliage is invaluable as a background for many mixed arrangements, it is perhaps best, when the flowers are in bloom, to use them alone and let nothing detract from their elegance. As the natural inclination of this shrub is a fall of flowers, I like to arrange them in a low, sweeping curve for which it is necessary to have a wide-lipped urn on a tall stem so that the branches can drop well down at the sides. I have used tall fruit bowls, and even old-fashioned cake-stands, to get the effect of a cascading bush of flowers.

Seed pods of *Dipelta floribunda* and green flowers of *Cornus kousa* form the outline in this mixed green group. The centre is filled in with hosta leaves, Corsican hellebores gone to seed, *Alchemilla mollis* and two large echeveria species.

Above: Orange-centred narcissi within the curve of stems of budding Horse Chestnut. The stones balance the weight of the heavy branches and fronds of a house plant fern are arranged between them.

Left: Pale mauve, leafless lilac arranged with grey eucalyptus foliage in an antique silver water-jug.

A single stem of purple-cupped *Magnolia* × *soulangiana* 'Lennei' standing in a modern pottery vase where it is seen to best advantage. This variety has exceptionally good lasting qualities.

Rhododendrons

Rhododendrons, rather like camellias, are generally seen to best advantage if arranged on their own. Many of the most spectacular are too big to mingle easily with other flowers, although a few heads can make a bold and colourful centre to a really big group. Among the more common varieties there are, however, a vast selection which provide lovely, rounded flowers invaluable in arrangements at this time. In gardens where the common mauve ponticum rhododendron grows in abundance, a striking arrangement can be made by stripping it of leaves and using it in conjunction with white and purple flag irises and any dark tulips, like the peony-flowered 'Clara Carder'. It must be remembered, however, that although these tones are memorable by day they lose their colour at night and should not be considered for an evening party.

Azaleas

Azaleas differ widely both in type and range of colour, but I have a special preference for the evergreen Japanese varieties whose purity of tone in shell-pink and rose blend so happily with lilacs and rhododendrons and make a setting of perfection for tree peonies. To the average person, however, I think the word 'Azalea' conjures up visions of sweet-scented shrubs blazing in shades of flame and yellow, the more brilliant of them having the effect of a light from within. Among the wild species, the Mollis and the Ghent (or so well-named 'Honeysuckle' azaleas), these colours predominate and the flowers are lavishly abundant, but as the majority of these types are deciduous they last less well when cut than the evergreen varieties. It is, therefore, advisable to use the latter where possible in conjunction with other flowers, and to keep the deciduous azaleas for arrangement on their own. It is always simpler to renew a whole group rather than remove fading, and possibly entangled, branches from among their longer-lasting companions. The fact that many azaleas are rather short-lived should not discourage us, however, from enjoying their beauty indoors, as the brilliance of their colour and the honey sweetness of their scent make them desirable for all occasions.

Magnolias

Magnolias are one of the most beautiful of all flowering trees, and each year I await their blossoming with increased excitement. The branches flow and curve in such a galaxy of design that no other adornment is really necessary, and they are worthy of alabaster or the most noble urn. Unfortunately the flowers bruise so easily that it is wisest to cut them while still in bud and let them open in water after the arrangement is completed. Most magnolias will last quite well indoors if treated with initial care except, unfortunately, the lovely waxy-petalled *M. stellata* which fades too quickly to justify cutting it for decorative purposes. The exquisite, purple-cupped *M. × soulangiana* 'Lennei' has exceptionally good lasting qualities, and in the illustration facing page 57 a single stem is shown standing in a modern pottery vase where the perfect leaf formation and purple bud, opening to display the inner pearl-white flower, are seen to best advantage.

Green flowers

Green is a colour which has a very subtle grace of its own, but we are apt to disregard it in springtime as we are still dazzled by the riot of colour which has followed the winter's bleakness. This is, perhaps, a pity, as at no other time of the year does green have quite the same limpid quality and pure clarity in all its variations. The L-shaped group facing page 56 was arranged in a small boat-shaped trough and had as its main outline two long stems of a Chinese shrub called *Dipelta floribunda*, which produces pale green, semi-transparent seed-pods when its flowers are over. Green flowers of *Cornus kousa*, Corsican hellebores gone to seed, lime-green *Alchemilla mollis* and feathery *Pelargonium crispum* 'Variegatum' completed the outline, while the more solid centre was formed with three echeveria species and variegated hosta leaves. Although the material used may sound unusual it was all gathered from my own and a near-by garden in late May, and in every garden and hedgerow there is other material for experiments of this kind, and beauty is to be found in unexpected places. A truly satisfying green group could be remembered long after the colourful ones of spring and summer were forgotten.

5. Summer Abundance

Amid the lavish splendour of summer flowers it is reasonable to discard caution and revel in the luxury of all that is at our disposal. The brilliance attained by an arrangement of flowers on their own is far more in accordance with the prodigality of summer than an arrangement where foliage is much in evidence. I do not mean by this that vases should be crammed with flowers; on the contrary, lightness and naturalness are as important now as at any other time, but greenery is no longer required for the sake of economy, or for lack of sufficient flowers, as it can be at other seasons.

Let us consider for a moment a few of the traditional flowers of summer. Roses, which to most of us come first in our affections from our earliest years, can be as prodigious in a cottage garden as in a great one; sweet peas bloom more abundantly when picked continually and fragrant pinks grow in such cushions of profusion that foliage is rarely seen. A herbaceous border can be literally a blaze of colour, and many of the summer-flowering shrubs drop such laden branches to the ground that they resemble coloured fountains.

Flowers appeal to us in a number of different ways. Some people love those that have obvious popularity, while others find enjoyment in rare varieties which are a test of ability to grow successfully and use with subtle skill in an arrangement. But, whichever way our taste lies, the extravagant glory of summer flowers fills our requirements. During these brief months we can indulge in our particular delights to the extent of intoxication and gain increasing knowledge in the furtherance of our quest for the beauty that enhances both our gardens and our homes.

In one brief chapter it is obviously impossible to extol more than a few of the abundant flowers of summer, and I must, therefore, confine myself to those that I have found particularly valuable in decoration and, perhaps understandably, those that are among my favourite flowers.

Roses

The first gathered handful of garden roses is, to most of us, the prelude to the joys of summer, heralding the advent of the multitudinous varieties of the rose and the flowering of delphiniums, peonies, poppies, Canterbury bells, old-fashioned Sweet Williams and sweet-scented stocks and pinks which are but a few of the well-known flowers we associate with the month of June.

There are so many different ways of using roses, and so many different types at our disposal, that it is difficult to know where to begin. Personally, I think they are unsurpassed in whatever manner they are used. Although some may be seen to best advantage if arranged on their own, others are essential factors in many decorative schemes. A rose itself is an object of such charm and beauty that it lends grace to any group of flowers where it displays itself, so that the inclusion of a few is to be recommended in most mixed arrangements during the weeks of their abundant flowering.

Most gardens contain rose trees of one kind or another. They may be modern roses—such as the hybrid teas, the showy floribundas or smaller polyanthus—the many species of climbers and ramblers or the older Bourbon roses, all of which are so variously and gloriously coloured and which flower so accommodatingly from June until the late autumn mists and frosts finally destroy them. These roses are the supreme joy of all flower arrangers, and now the increasing popularity of the real 'old' roses has added a further undreamed-of pleasure for those who have opportunity and space in which to grow them. In my own garden my collection of these 'old' roses is creeping insidiously into areas destined for other purposes, but they have an undefinable charm which I am powerless to resist. All are so deliciously scented that the air around them is filled with fragrance and their colours range from white through clear, silvery pinks to the more muted tones of lilac, purple and maroon, some of which are clearly striped with deeper tones or shaded as if with a paint brush. Their style is also a decorator's dream, being flat and rounded with double or semi-double petals disposed in the manner of a camellia, while the outer petals of many curve inwards like a shallow cup to enclose all those that lie within. Although the flowering period of the 'old' shrub roses is mainly restricted to June and July, the pleasure derived from them more than warrants their inclusion in any garden where there is space available to allow for their prodigious growth.

Summer roses are shown in mixed arrangements in the illustrations between pages 72 and 73, facing page 65, and on their own in the picture of the little Rockingham figure pushing the laden wheelbarrow shown facing page 73. The first arrangement was a collection of early summer flowers in tones of shell-pink, lilac and varied blues. The only foliage used was lime branches stripped entirely of leaves, as the pale green of the lime flowers acted as a foil to the clear colours of the flowers. The outline was formed with 'Peach-blossom' gladioli, delphiniums and lilac stocks, while two be-flowered stems of the delicately pretty little shell pink cabbage rose 'De Meaux' formed the centre, together with single and double peonies of almost the same soft tone. Long-stemmed lilac sweet peas followed a line through the group from left to right to flow down at one side, and trailing stems of pink *Escallonia* × *ingramii* gave emphasis to the downward curving design which is desirable for any arrangement which is raised on a pedestal.

The second group shows the brilliance of mixed red flowers, so many tones of which can be blended most happily (and surprisingly) together. Here, again, a spray of roses formed the centre, but in this case it was a floribunda. On the left is a stem of the Gallica rose, 'Cardinal de Richelieu', which has purple petals tinged with the grey bloom of a grape, while on both sides is another of the 'old' roses, a moss named 'Maréchal Davoust', whose deep pink tones blended with those of the pelargoniums near it. Crimson geraniums, vivid red modern 'Baccara' roses, puce stock, deep red single peonies, stems of red *Escallonia* × *langleyensis* and honeysuckle buds mingled with the quieter grey buds of *Hosta sieboldiana* and a velvet *Begonia rex* leaf to bring together such a medley of rich tones and sweet scents that both the eyes and nose were captivated. The dark blue-grey background, the soft patina on the polished table, and the gleam of the antique gilt frame above provided a setting that seemed completely satisfying for this particular arrangement.

Roses are also included in the basket of late summer flowers facing page 64, but this is in quite a different style. A bright mixture of garden flowers generally looks best in a simple container, and the rush-coloured background did not detract from the gay colours. A basket should, I think, look full of flowers—as if it had, in fact, been brought in from the garden—and for this reason the handle should remain in evidence. These are the types of flowers that might be found in any garden during September: dahlias, zinnias, African marigolds, geraniums and spiky stems of mont-bretia, with roses new and 'old'. There is a 'Queen Elizabeth' rose tucked into the middle, with sprays of the lovely white bourbon rose 'Boule de Neige' above it, and to the right, sprays of rose hips and silvery *Senecio cineraria*. The pale green tassels of amaranthus (a green version of the crimson type known as 'Love-Lies-Bleeding') and lime-flowered cypress spurge (*Euphorbia cyparissias*), set off the bright, clear colours of the flowers, with the result that they mixed as happily indoors as in their natural environment.

The perfection of roses is shown, I think, ideally in the picture facing page 73 where the tiny porcelain wheelbarrow is filled to overflowing with the miniature rose 'Cecile Brunner'. These minute flowers are no bigger than a sixpence, with buds and foliage in proportion, and each bloom is a perfect replica of the normal sized flowers of their genus. Similar small arrangements would look enchanting as individual decorations on a dinner table. Admittedly Rockingham figures cannot be bought by the dozen, but there are many small inexpensive pieces of modern pottery which would serve the purpose just as well.

Before I leave roses for other flowers I would like to say a few words about their care. It is generally advisable to pick them while still in full bud, as their life is not long once they are fully open. Thorns and lower leaves are best removed, and the stems should be split or crushed and the flowers placed in deep water for several hours before being arranged. If the heads droop they can be rolled in paper for their whole length, but this applies to long-stemmed shop roses rather than to the garden variety. When roses have been arranged it is often necessary to cut away leaves that may detract from the beauty and colour of the flower, and heavily beflowered branches of climbers or 'old' shrub roses will remain useful longer if blooms are removed when they fade, as opening buds will take their place.

Peonies

Herbaceous peonies are among the loveliest and most useful of summer flowers for indoor decoration. The flowers are borne on long, slender stems which can be induced to curve in any direction, while the full, rounded heads make a perfect centre for any arrangement (see the illustrations facing page 65 and between pages 72 and 73). They are equally beautiful on their own, particularly if arranged in the manner of the cascading design described in Chapter 2. The double varieties last longer than the single types, but the latter are so exquisite that their inclusion in a group is worth while even if they must be renewed occasionally during the life of their more stalwart companions. These border peonies flower prolifically when once established (which may take a year or more) and they like good, rich soil.

The spectacular tree peonies are more difficult to grow and a late frost can annihilate the tender shoots which may have advanced too far in the delusion that summer is near. A little protection from cold winds, and also shade from the misleading sun of March and April, is therefore advisable as the flowers themselves are of quite unparalleled beauty. Despite their perfection as blooms, tree peonies are not easy to show adequately in decorations, as the large, and often heavy, heads are borne on soft, short stems and nestle among their own leaves. For this reason many require support when cut, and are best used at the heart of an arrangement among fragile blossom such as azalea, stripped philadelphus or garden lilac. Possibly because some forms resemble a water-lily, a single bloom can be shown lying among its own leaves in a shallow dish where every exquisite detail of its structure can be seen.

The colours of herbaceous peonies range mainly from white through all shades of silvery pink to red and crimson, but the colours of tree peonies are infinitely more varied and include those of cream, golden yellow and apricot as well as combinations of two or even more colours. Perhaps because my personal preference leans always towards pale, clear tones I find the white and soft shell-pink varieties most satisfying. There is some ethereal quality in the silken petals of tree peonies which is more evident, to me at least, in such types as Yano Okima (pure white), Horaisan (clear pink) or Haru-ne-akebono (white with pink centre), and it is these I would like to grow successfully.

63

A MEDLEY OF FLOWERS

This showy mixture of summer flowers includes a number of varieties common to most gardens. Colours are strong in August and September, and many a herbaceous border will have massed flowers similar to these. Pink, vermilion, orange, yellow, shades of mauve and a touch of scarlet will all blend while growing together and only require the cool effect of green or grey to restore harmony when such contrasting flowers are brought indoors.

It is satisfying at times to gather just such a gay mixture, and a basket is a very suitable container for an arrangement which displays so many different types of garden flowers. It should look, I feel, rather casually overcrowded, as this is not the time for elegant lines or carefully studied positions. Too meticulous grouping might have detracted from the natural effect, but it will be seen that I have used the paler colours for the outline and kept the strongest colours and largest flowers for the centre.

In this garden medley there are roses, geraniums, dahlias, marigolds, zinnias, spikes of montbretia, rose hips and hydrangea, while the necessary green and grey has been added by cypress spurge, green tassels of *Amaranthus caudatus* and silvery *Senecio cineraria*. The only unusual flower among these garden favourites is the montbretia-like spike at the top centre of the arrangement. This is a *Watsonia* from South Africa and is worth growing for its exceptionally long-lasting qualities and also because of the brilliance of its intense orange-flame colouring.

Zinnias are, I think, one of the most valuable annuals for the flower arranger owing to their wide colour range and uniformly round formation. In addition to the many bright varieties, which are well known, there are also the most subtle shades of rose pink, buff apricot, lemon and greenish white which are, unfortunately, too rarely seen. The variety 'Peppermint Stick', as its name implies, has flowers striped in many shades. I also grow the dwarf variety 'Thumbelina', as these tiny flowers are exquisitely perfect in miniature groups.

MIXED RED FLOWERS

Red flowers have a dramatic quality and also a great attraction. Daring effects can be obtained by mixing such contrasting shades as rose with flame, puce with scarlet or magenta with maroon. On this occasion, however, I felt there was no need for drama as the clear colours of the flowers had a brilliance of their own and required no shock tactics to emphasize their charm. 'Old' roses mingled with more modern floribunda and hybrid tea roses to add a touch of sumptuous richness with their velvet purple bloom; startling red geraniums, rosy pelargoniums, crimson peonies with golden stamens and deep pink stock combined together to give an effect of brilliant red.

The foliage is, perhaps, unusual as the red escallonia, *E. × langleyensis*, is less well known than the pink varieties. Such strong-coloured flowers could have looked heavy but the trailing stems of this lovely shrub lent grace and lightness to the whole arrangement. The honeysuckle comes from a small bush in my garden which grows in the manner of a weeping standard rose tree, the main stem being formed initially by the intertwining of several stems round a short post. In mid-summer it is covered completely in deep red buds which open later into yellow honeysuckle flowers. The curious grey buds at the top of the arrangement are from a plantain lily, *Hosta sieboldiana*, and I have used them here to strike a quiet note among such brilliant colours. The *Begonia rex* leaf was added to repeat the velvet-like texture of the 'old' roses which is apparent in the deep purple 'Cardinal de Richelieu' and the lighter-toned 'Maréchal Davoust'.

When this group was completed it seemed to me that a dark bluegrey background was required. There was nothing suitable in my own house, where white walls predominate, and therefore the help of friends was enlisted and flowers, camera, and all those concerned were transported to a lovely Georgian house where just such a background existed. The extra trouble involved was well repaid as at once the flowers looked at home.

Poppies and lupins

Both annual and perennial poppies are unfortunately short-lived indoors, but they will last longer if they are picked while still in bud and their stems immersed momentarily in boiling water as described on page 14, Chapter 2. Annual Shirley poppies have such a wide range of colour and so many different flower styles that they are well worth the extra trouble needed in preparing them. But it is, I think, advisable to arrange them on their own, using all varieties of colour, which never seem to clash, and to enjoy them for some special occasion, such as a luncheon or dinner party, rather than risk disappointment when they fail as a more perpetual decoration. The perennial oriental poppies, being more sturdy, will last a day or two when cut if treated in the same way. The white, black-centred variety combines well with peonies and many types of blossom. There is also an exquisitely beautiful Californian tree poppy named *Romneya coulteri*, which is a cross between a shrub and a herbaceous plant. This has large white flowers, similar to a single-petalled peony, with a central crown of golden stamens. Although it lasts, unfortunately, no longer than others of its kind, its unique beauty warrants its inclusion in certain delicate arrangements.

Lupins, which are so effective in the garden and are now so varied in their colours, are apt to be disappointing when brought indoors. The stems may curl and twist in a multitude of ways and the petals drop almost overnight. Nevertheless, they can be enjoyed rather briefly as a decoration if given the hot-water treatment and arranged entirely on their own, as the stems can then make their own design in a manner that is not unpleasing. I do not think they are flowers to use in a mixed arrangement as they neither last nor keep their shape long enough to warrant the time needed for arranging them in this way.

Flowers suitable for outlines

It is generally necessary to have a few tapered flowers to form the 'spine' in a mixed arrangement and also to indicate the outline, provided the flowers are not too stiff and upright in their manner of growth, in which case it is inadvisable to place them at angles or horizontally.

Foxgloves (Digitalis) are among the first of the elegant tall spikes which are useful for this purpose. There are now many hybrids available which are entirely different in form and colour from the original spikes carrying pink and white drooping bell-like flowers so familiar in shady or woodland places. Whatever their form may be, however, I think foxgloves are best used in an upright position, as this is the manner of their growth.

Delphiniums, on the other hand, are more adaptable, perhaps because they are fuller in shape, and slender, arching side-shoots can be found which conform to any design. I find these flowers unrivalled for outline work as they give a light and delicate air to any arrangement, either large or small, and white delphiniums have an aura of starry freshness similar to blossom and so should be used, whenever available, among all white flowers. Mixed blue delphiniums are used to outline the group pictured between pages 72 and 73, and the many hybrids include tones of pink and primrose and even shades of rosy-lilac which are subtle enough to blend with a 'Prelude' rose. Delphiniums have hollow, rather brittle, stems and require a long drink in deep water before being arranged. As with most flowers the medium or smaller types are more useful for decoration indoors than the over-large specimen blooms. There are always exceptions, however, and I remember a vast group of specimen blue delphiniums which was arranged in front of a mirror with no extraneous foliage and only giant grey artichoke leaves and pale blue hydrangeas to give emphasis to the more solid centre. Some of the spires were so tall that the hollow stems bent under the weight of flowers and it was necessary to support them for part of their length by the insertion of slender sticks which in no way harmed the flowers themselves.

Eremurus (the Foxtail Lilies) are excellent for really big arrangements, but I find they are more elegant if confined to the 'spine' of an arrangement as they are essentially upright, stately flowers. The long stiff stems are terminated by torch-like spikes of white, yellow, pink or pale apricot flowers, and they last a long time in water which mitigates against their rather high cost. Although they are considered to be hardy perennials they are not very easy to grow, so it is, perhaps, better to buy them when there is a good choice available during June and July. Eremurus are shown in the church decorations pictured between pages 136 and 137.

Gladioli have the longest season, and of all pointed summer flowers are among the most numerous in colour and form. They are seen in shop windows from early spring until November and, because they continue to flower in gardens in the rotation in which they are planted, varieties are constantly available to the decorator. The large-flowered varieties are invaluable for big groups, and provided they are not grown specifically for market, where straightness is desired, many have graceful, curving stems which can form a firm outline for a big design. For smaller arrangements I prefer the newer dwarf types, as they have slender stems which are more easy to handle than their larger, stiff-stemmed predecessors. I find the small varieties such as 'The Bride' (pure white), 'Peachblossom' (rosy pink) and 'Charm' (lilac) among the most useful, as they are unmarked by a super-imposed colour as distinct from many other small types. It is generally advisable to place a second, shorter stem of gladiolus in front of the first, as the opening buds will then cover the fading ones of the flower directly behind it. I have always found these dying flowerets a problem, as their removal can leave a length of bare stem which will spoil a group of mixed flowers that is otherwise still pleasing.

Stocks are among my favourite flowers. They are so varied in their colours that they blend with any scheme and are heavily scented until they grow old. The long double varieties are particularly useful as the stems are flexible, and I use them to outline designs and fill in backgrounds in arrange-ments both great and small for as long as they are procurable. The leaves are apt to be rather coarse and last less well than the flowers, so it is advisable to remove all the lower ones and to thin out the top ones to some degree. The thick, woody stems require crushing or splitting. Stocks are illustrated in the arrangement between pages 72 and 73.

Antirrhinums are useful background flowers provided they are long enough. Although they are usually grown as a rather bushy half-hardy annual, some of the tall varieties can be as long as three feet; at this size, however, they are apt to be rather spidery, so several stems of varying lengths should be inserted at the same base to get the required effect in colour.

Pentstemons are slightly similar to antirrhinums but are restricted in their colour, which ranges from white through pink to scarlet and purple.

They are useful for smallish arrangements as they have spikes of neat tubular flowers.

The feathery plumes of astilbes can be beautiful in some arrangements but are apt to be fussy in others. They require as companions, I think, clear-cut, waxy flowers such as lilies or galtonias, when the combination can be very lovely indeed. I grow pink and white varieties near a pond as they prefer moist places.

The bright yellow, orange or scarlet poker-shaped spikes of kniphofias (tritomas) lend elegance to groups of late summer flowers, where their brilliance is reflected in the equally bright colours of zinnias and dahlias. There are pale varieties, and also small, delicate species, such as *K. galpinii*, all of which are valuable assets at a time when pointed flowers are becoming increasingly scarce.

Flowers for centres and focal points

Although rounded flowers are generally required for the centres of most arrangements, particularly for those of mixed flowers, it should not be assumed that they are essential any more than that pointed flowers are always required to form an outline. But it does simplify the pattern of a decoration if certain types of flowers are allocated to these positions, if only for experimental purposes. It is, I think, the quality of the flower which is important, by which I mean that a stem of lilies might, for instance, be regarded as tapering in form and yet its character induces one to place it in the most noticeable position.

In general, however, some rounded flowers are necessary to create visual balance, without which a group can appear unsteady. Peonies, as already mentioned, are perfect for this purpose and there are a host of other summer flowers which have the same effect. Carnations are a good example, as their perfect, uniformly round blooms are carried on such long, thin stems that they conform to any desired design. Like roses and spray chrysanthemums they are available throughout the year and, perhaps because of this, are regarded as expensive flowers and rarely seen in sufficient quantity. This is a pity and should be remedied in the summer, which is their proper season, as their richness and scent are more apparent when they are arranged in a lavish manner. Their range of colour is wide, and there are many that are striped and shaded in the manner of the 'old' roses, with which they associate well, while the many red varieties, ranging from clove to the 'shocking pink' of 'Winonah' give a brilliance to a mixed red group which is often difficult to find among other flowers. When they are arranged by themselves I think it is desirable to place them among foliage which is similar in colour to their own grey foliage, as the latter is, unfortunately, rarely procurable. *Senecio laxifolius* or *Senecio leucostachys* are among those suitable in the summer, and eucalyptus or silver grevillea are useful in the winter.

There are a number of annuals and biennials which provide lovely rounded flowers, among which zinnias are some of the most useful as their colour range is so wide. The large varieties have a bad habit of strangling themselves, as the top-heavy heads can bend over on the hollow stems before sufficient water is absorbed. This can be prevented by the insertion of a wire through the head as shown in Chapter 2, Figure 16. Most good flower shops wire zinnias in this way before selling them.

The common marguerites and South African arctotis are attractive daisy-like flowers which are useful among the lighter, fluffier annuals such as larkspur. Gerberas are an exotic type of South African daisy and are seen more often in the shops during the winter months than growing in British gardens. But *G. jamesonii* can be grown with initial greenhouse protection, and the exquisite colours are an asset to decoration as there are tones and variations on the theme of ivory through buff and salmon to flame and orange which are more subtle than any I know, while some shades of pink rival those of anthuriums.

Although it may seem a far cry from gerberas to marigolds (calendulas), these gay flowers play a big part in summer arrangements. I find the sturdy lemon and orange pompon African marigolds particularly useful as they last well when cut and mix most happily with the clear bright colours of late summer flowers. All plants commonly called 'marigold' do not necessarily belong to the same family and these big African marigolds are called *Tagetes erecta*. Both types are easy flowers to grow and should find a place in every garden.

There are other types of plants with trusses of small flowers bunched on to a single stem which, although not uniformly rounded in shape, are nevertheless suitable for the centres and focal points of decorations, as their structure gives the necessary appearance of solidity.

Geraniums and regal pelargoniums are examples and can be seen in the mixed red group facing page 65 and also massed together in the illustration on page 80.

I feel these flowers need a note of explanation because most people refer to the popular summer-bedding plant, a zonal-leaved pelargonium, as a 'geranium' whereas this name really belongs to a hardy herbaceous perennial which is generally blue in colour. However, I doubt if this muddle in nomenclature will stop the average person from thinking of a pelargonium as a geranium but, for the record, the common bedding variety is a zonal pelargonium, the trailing type an ivy-leaved pelargonium and the showy greenhouse plant, commonly considered to be simply a pelargonium, is, in fact, a regal pelargonium.

I use 'geraniums' on many occasions in decorations as they add a brilliance to pink and red arrangements which is hard to find among other flowers. They are, however, perhaps most effective when arranged on their own, as their spectacular range of colour from palest shell-pink through every shade of scarlet to 'shocking pink' and deepest crimson never seem to clash unpleasingly when massed together.

Geraniums cannot stand much handling and I find it best to dispense with the usual preliminary drink in deep water and to arrange them immediately in the vase where they will remain. Treated in this manner their lasting powers are considerable.

Border phlox and Sweet Williams are other flowers whose structure make them suitable for focal points, and the many hybrid alstroemerias are invaluable as they last extremely well when cut and those in shades of apricot, salmon pink and flame are particularly beautiful and much lighter in form than the original speckled orange variety which I do not find inspiring.

Alliums, too, come in this category, and the lilac tones mix well among quiet-coloured flowers. Alliums are also valuable for their seed-heads.

Agapanthus are useful in large arrangements, as the fine heads of small lily-like flowers are carried on long leafless stems which mitigate against any effect of heaviness. *A. orientalus* (deep blue) grows out of doors suc-

71

cessfully in my garden and there is also a lovely white variety which gives airiness to groups that include more solid flowers.

Lilies

I began this chapter with roses and I end my list with lilies which, to me, are likewise in a class apart from other flowers. A stem of lilies lends a touch of distinction to any arrangement and I try, whenever possible, to include a few in church decorations or in any group where dignity and grace should be a ruling factor. Because lilies are, perforce, exceptional flowers, they should be placed where their elegance shows to best advantage. Well-known lilies, such as the white *L. longiflorum* and *L. formosanum*, the faintly pink-tinged *L. regale* and the huge golden *L. auratum,* all of which have trumpet-shaped flowers on budded stems, look their best in mixed arrangements when carried in a curving line from the top of the arrangement to the down-flowing central stem. If only a few are available I place them high and in the centre of a group, one below the other, but never tucked in low as lilies can lose their personality if deprived of their characteristic stems. All the above have the typical sweet, heavy scent associated with lilies, and *L. candidum* (the white Madonna lily which flourishes in gardens great and small) is as deliciously scented as any of them. This, however, is a rather stiff and upright-growing variety and should be treated accordingly when arranged indoors. It would be impossible to indicate in one short paragraph the many complex varieties of lilies and I have, therefore, confined myself to mentioning some of those most commonly seen in shops or grown in gardens, but the principles suggested for their use in decoration apply to others of their genus. It is, unfortunately, necessary as a rule to remove the caps from the stamens of lilies, as the pollen can stain the surrounding petals and also anything else with which it comes in contact. Although this does detract in some measure from the character of the flower itself, it is preferable to having blotched petals and stained clothes.

Green and grey plants and leaves

During these months, when the emphasis is mainly on flowers and foliage is temporarily forgotten, there still remains the necessity for the introduc-

Flowering crab-apple (*Malus hupehensis*) with azaleas and *Viburnum plicatum tomentosum* in the centre of this elongated arrangement.

Above: Blue irises and palm stems rising from a base of *Begonia rex* leaves.
Right: A collection of early summer flowers in tones of shell-pink, lilac and varied blues were used in this downward curving arrangement designed to stand on a pedestal.

This small porcelain wheelbarrow is filled with the miniature rose 'Cecile Brunner', the flowers of which are the size of a sixpence with buds and foliage in proportion.

tion of green or grey as quiet colours to offset the brilliance of surrounding flowers. This is the time, therefore, when leaves can be used most successfully and some of the unusual green and grey plants become exceptionally valuable.

Hostas (which were previously known as 'funkias') are an important adjunct to any decorator's garden and many are prodigious growers when once established. The leaves, which are of primary importance for decoration, grow larger under moist and slightly shaded conditions. The glaucous, blue-grey leaves of *H. sieboldiana* are, perhaps, the best known, and their lilac-white flowers have a curious distinction especially when still partially in bud. *H. crispula* is, to me, the most spectacular, with long, pointed green leaves boldly outlined in white, and *H. fortunei* 'Albopicta' is one of the most colourful as it has creamy-coloured leaves edged with pale green. *H. fortunei*, although less showy than others of its kind, is more prolific and one can pick the sage-green leaves with impunity.

The thick, rounded leaves of bergenias are always useful and last for weeks in water. I am, however, inclined to let them rest during the summer when so many other types are available, as they come into their own during the autumn and winter months when many assume lovely burnished tones.

The grey prickly leaves of the biennial onopordons (the Scot's Thistle) provide effective contrast in pastel-coloured arrangements. I find them more useful for decoration during their first year, when the leaves are smaller and easier to handle. These thick, hairy leaves are apt to syphon in the same manner as *Stachys olympica* (better known as *S. lanata*), so it is advisable to trim those parts which will be in water of any prickles or flounces that adhere to them and to make sure that the leaves are dry before insertion in a vase.

The giant, statuesque divided leaves of the globe artichoke lend great elegance to large arrangements. They need a preliminary long drink in deep water, after which they are remarkably long-lasting, provided a few inches of their stems lie well below the water-level. The 'Cardoons' (*Cynara* species) are closely related, but are even more deeply serrated and produce thistles rather than edible heads which make them preferable (and less wasteful) for decorative purposes. With both types it is necessary to place them in position before filling the vase with other material, as their stems are so thick and fleshy that later insertion would be almost impossible.

A sowing of decorative kale in spring is also a useful addition to a 'picking garden', as these colourful plants become available when the hostas are fading and provide leaves of many different formations and varied colours for winter decoration. The colours range from white, edged green, through cream and shades of pink to purple, and sizes vary from minute, often immensely ornate, leaves to those large enough for pedestal groups. Deep cream and green kale leaves are shown arranged with the beautiful new, double freesia 'Fantasy' in the illustration facing page 16. As the lasting power of kale is considerable, one is tempted to leave it too long in a vase when the cabbage smell can become apparent. This can be checked to some extent by a few small lumps of charcoal in the water but, as the plants throw out new leaves continually, it is better to replace any offending leaves with fresh ones.

The placing of leaves in decoration is, of course, a matter of personal taste and suitability to the required shape. In arrangements where the focal point is central I find that they are most effective if placed in a group of from two to five leaves in a basal position directly in line with the 'spine' of the arrangement. From here they should stem from one point in the manner of flower petals, as shown in Figures 22 and 23. On those occasions when the emphasis is to the side, as in L-shaped arrangements, then the leaves should be placed at the base of, and directly behind, the vertical stem in order to balance the long horizontal arm. (See Figure 23.)

Among the smaller grey foliage plants, *Senecio laxifolius*, *Stachys olym-*

FIGURE 22   FIGURE 23

74

pica and *Senecio cineraria* are all fairly well known and play an important part in decoration among the clear-toned flowers of summer. I also grow *Convolvulous cneorum*, which has the most beautiful little silken grey leaves imaginable, but it is not an easy plant to grow as it requires much warmth and perfect drainage. On the other hand, the little evergreen grey plant, *Othonnopsis cheirifolia*, which has paddle-shaped leaves on trailing stems, does well with me and is useful at times when other more delicate grey plants are hard to come by.

Some green plants can take their place in arrangements as either flowers or foliage, among which are *Euphorbia venator* (grown in gardens as *E. wulfenii*) and 'Solomon's Seal'. These are as effective in their green state as when they bear their small greenish flowers. The lime-green leaves and tiny feathery lime-coloured flower sprays of *Alchemilla mollis* give a cool effect to vivid early summer flowers, and later on the green variety of *Amaranthus caudatus* repeats the same lime tinge in its flowing tasselled sprays. Sedums provide a variety of different greens and are well worth growing in sunny places. The large 'ice plant' *S. spectabile* is, perhaps, the most useful, as the thick, fleshy pale green stems last a long time in water and are, I think, more effective as green plants than when crowned with flat heads of mauvy-pink flowers. Variegated ivies are well-known as pot plants, but certain types can also be grown out of doors where they can be cut for use in decoration. I grow 'Silver Queen', which is a small-leaved ivy often streaked with pink, and also the larger *Hedera canariensis* 'Variegata', both of which do well against a north wall.

Two annuals are well worth growing for green decoration, namely, *Euphorbia marginata*, a long-stemmed plant crowned with variegated green and white flowers, and *Moluccella laevis* ('Bells of Ireland'), the clear green bells of which are borne on long stems and are as lovely in a green or white group as among the most brilliant flowers. I also grow a geranium called 'Happy Thought', as the clear green and white foliage is useful in many small arrangements.

Summer-flowering shrubs

Trees and shrubs play an important part among flowers in their natural setting, so that the introduction of a few sprays of summer blossom

75

in the larger type of decorations is well worth while.

It would, of course, be impossible to give anything like a comprehensive list in the space available, but I would like to suggest a few of the varieties which I have found especially useful. Although I have already mentioned philadelphus in a preceding chapter, it rightly belongs here as some varieties flower well into July. I find all types desirable, from the small, creamy and strongly fragrant original 'Mock Orange' to the fluffy rosettes and large camellia-like flowers of more recent hybrids. Double-flowered philadelphus, including the extremely fragrant hybrid 'Virginal', forms the outline for the church decoration illustrated between pages 136 and 137. When flowing stems of this lovely shrub are arranged with white delphiniums, Madonna lilies and white peonies, they form together an arrangement which, in grace, scent and delicacy of form, interprets for me the essential spirit of midsummer.

Escallonias are useful because of the arching manner of their growth and are illustrated in both the summer groups described in this chapter.

Stephanandra tanakae is one of the most lovely shrubs for indoor decoration as it throws out long, arching stems covered in lace-like panicles of creamy flowers which last a long time when cut. It is exceptionally beautiful among yellow flowers and even more so among those of cream and gold. As I do not grow this shrub myself I am unfamiliar with its habits, but it grows in profusion in a near-by garden.

The kalmias flower during June and I find the shell-pink variety K. *latifolia* most useful. The heads of its small, compact flowers are rounded, so this shrub is useful for central points.

The pointed spikes of buddleia are useful in shape for many arrangements, but the rather hard mauve colour is difficult to blend with summer flowers. There are, however, white varieties, such as 'Peace', which are particularly effective among other white flowers as their leaves are backed with silvery grey.

Ceanothus, although not very long-lasting when cut, is useful because blue is a rare colour among shrubs. I have a decidous variety called 'Gloire de Versailles' which is covered in long sprays of fluffy, powder-blue flowers in July and August, and later the red-brown seed-heads are effective in autumn groups.

Hydrangeas are, of course, among the most generally useful of all summer shrubs as they flower from July until late autumn and provide rounded heads in a wonderful variety of both clear and subtle colours. The lacecaps are, as their name implies, a lighter and more delicate-looking species which I find invaluable in decoration. *H. paniculata* is quite different in form, as the creamy heads are pointed and the tips are finally flushed with pink. Although this variety flourishes quite well in my garden it bears no resemblance to my first sight of this shrub in Scotland, where enormous long stems lifted their torch-like heads towards the sky. I suppose our damp climate is not quite damp enough. All hydrangeas require a lot of water and can absorb moisture through their heads as well as through their stems. If they show signs of wilting while being given their preliminary long drink it is helpful to cover their heads with damp tissue paper. The heads can also be lightly sprayed when once they are in position if there is any doubt about them lasting under especially warm conditions.

In order to capture the beauty of summer flowers one would need a photographer perpetually at one's elbow, but photography sessions have to be planned in advance and flowers neither wait for nor bloom at pre-arranged dates. The majority of flowers illustrated in this book, and certainly most of those in this chapter, have, therefore, been gathered in my own or near-by gardens, as good photography shows not only the perfection of all it depicts but also the smallest blemish, and even the hardiest flowers lose a little of their pristine beauty when they have travelled far. Inevitably, as a result, examples have been missed. My tree peonies were imperfect when other flowers were at their best; blossom, being late this year, did not flower in time with its required companions and many of my favourite roses, both new and 'old', were either over or in bud when the camera was at hand. This is an explanation and not necessarily an apologia, as I hope the illustrations will show a pattern of flowers in which those that are omitted can later find a place.

6. Autumn Harmony

As the year fades the colours change. The bright clear tones of spring and summer give way to warmer shades and there is mellowness in the ripened fruits and berries and the splendour of autumnal leaves. Blue has almost gone, except in late hydrangeas, but the varied mauves of michaelmas daisies, like the mists which cloud the ground at this time, soften the richness of autumn colours.

Some flowers are now perennially with us, and so are colours which hitherto were associated with other seasons. Our one-time tawny chrysan-themums can now be as delicately pink as a peony or, in snowy whiteness and tones of clearest yellow, are often reminiscent of early spring. But do not imagine for an instant that such perpetual flowers, with their incredible range of colour, are unwelcome. On the contrary, like roses and carnations, they add immeasurably to the scope of our decorations during difficult months. I only plead that we remember the suitability of their natural shades during these weeks of autumn, when their golds and bronzes and tawny yellows mingle so happily with the changing scene around them.

It is easy sometimes, at this period of the year, to let a heaviness descend upon arrangements. Green is perhaps more necessary now than at any other time, in order to act as a high-light to the deeper tones. A group that has reddening leaves for a background of tawny flowers needs pale green among them, just as autumnal woods need fields to emphasize their glory. There is much to be found that is suitable. Ferns are excellent and a variety are worth growing in some shady place. The tall fronds of lime-green osmunda are more lovely than any other and, if given the hot-water treat-ment, will last reasonably well. I take a can of really hot water around when I pick them and this immediate immersion seems to increase their staying power considerably. Alternatively, if a spare bath is available, complete immersion overnight in cold water is probably the best treatment of all.

The sword-like leaves of New Zealand flax (*Phormium tenax*) edged in cream, and the lime-coloured spears of the giant montbretias, are both extremely useful. So, too, are the green husks of chestnuts on bare branches, trails of hops or green amaranthus, from both of which it is advisable to remove the leaves, and 'Old Man's Beard' before the seed-heads assume the fluffy greyness their name implies. The addition of any of these pale green foliages will give lightness to an autumnal group and emphasize the splendour of changing leaves in a way no darker foliage can do.

The reddening leaves, berries and late roses shown in the group facing page 81 were picked in mid-October and are typical of the warm tones seen at this time of the year. They are arranged in a tall alabaster urn, as height was necessary to display the drooping branches of berries and also the grace of 'Old Man's Beard', the stems of which are remarkably wiry and retain their shape indefinitely.

Stems of blazing orange-red hips of *Rosa moyesii* on the left, and cotoneaster with wild euonymus (spindle berry) on the right, formed the basis of the cascading design, but these almost leafless branches would have appeared hard without the softness lent by the following trails of 'Old Man's Beard'. Reddening azalea and peony foliage formed the 'spine', while on the right are flaming leaves of *Acer japonicum* 'Aconitifolium'. These autumn colours were repeated in the salmon-coloured roses, those named 'Queen' forming the outline and a floribunda named 'Spartan' forming the centre. The cool effect of green was introduced with the hydrangea.

This particular arrangement is an example of the relationship between flowers and their setting, as the warm tones blended with the velvet curtains while the opaque ivory tones of the alabaster urn made the whole arrangement stand out in relief from the panelling behind it. Autumn flowers look beautiful on occasions when arranged in containers of gleaming copper or bronze, but on this occasion copper would have detracted from the harmony between flowers and curtains, and bronze would have disappeared into the dark background.

ZONAL PELARGONIUMS

Zonal pelargoniums, more commonly called geraniums, are generally regarded as summer bedding plants rather than as flowers for
indoor decoration but, nevertheless, they have great value for the
latter use. In this arrangement many varieties have been massed
together in a glass fruit dish and it can be seen that the colours blend
most pleasingly despite the fact that shell and salmon-pink, scarlet,
puce and 'shocking pink' have all been included.

Geraniums are, perhaps, seen at their best when massed either in
one variety or many and are particularly effective as a table decoration where the general shortness of their stems is not a disadvantage.

I always grow a geranium with ornamental foliage (in this case
'Caroline Schmidt') as the cool effect of the green and white leaves
tones down the brilliant colours of other types and yet is equally
beautiful when used with a very pale pink geranium such as 'Lady
Stanley'. Other varieties used in this arrangement were 'Double
Jacoby' ('shocking pink'), 'Queen of Denmark' (salmon pink), and
a delicate mauve-pink ivy-leaved variety called 'Mrs. Martin'.

It is wisest to handle geraniums as little as possible and these flowers
came straight from the garden into the bowl. If left untouched
geraniums are remarkably long-lasting but when fully open the
petals shatter all too easily if disturbed.

LATE ROSES AMONG BERRIES AND AUTUMN LEAVES

The warm tones of autumn show best, I think, in a mellowed setting and nothing is more perfect for background than old panelling.

While searching for inspiration among reddening leaves, berries and the last of the garden flowers, I came upon some floribunda roses which were still blooming profusely. Among these the deep salmon-coloured 'Spartan' gave me the idea for this group and recalled to mind velvet curtains of a similar shade which adorned a panelled room in a friend's house. Within minutes a date was fixed, as the life of garden flowers is brief at this time, and shortly afterwards, with all the impedimenta of photographic equipment, we took possession momentarily of a lovely house.

This richly coloured group was arranged in a tall-stemmed alabaster *tazza* as it provided the height necessary to display the trailing stems of berries which are so typical of the autumn scene. The marquetry table was chosen because it stood out in greater contrast to the linenfold panelling than a darker one would have done and, being small, did not interrupt the flowing lines of the arrangement, which dropped below table level.

Because the berried branches were comparatively leafless, long trails of Old Man's Beard (the wild clematis of the hedgerows) were added to soften the outline, which was formed on the left by the giant scarlet hips from a *Rosa moyesii* and on the right by cotoneaster and wild euonymus. Reddening azalea and peony foliage are in the centre, while a stem of blazing *Acer japonicum* flows down on the right.

Despite the speed with which the date for photography was made, only a few 'Spartan' roses still retained their perfection, so these were used centrally as the main feature and were supplemented by market roses named 'Queen' which were almost identical in colour. A few rather over-blown 'Korona' floribundas gave the necessary depth, while two stems of pale green hydrangea added an appearance of weight and introduced again the cool tone of 'Old Man's Beard' which high-lighted the rich shades of flowers, leaves and berries.

Colours are not necessarily all so rich, and the quiet tones of michaelmas daisies are equally in keeping with the autumn scene. These flowers have a cloud-like appearance in the border when all the greyish-white, pink and lavender tones are intermingled, but it is difficult to reproduce this delicate effect indoors. I find it best to arrange them in a casual manner, taking in the whole range of their colours, and to place them against a window where the light shining through their feathery heads gives the misty effect they have in growth.

My thoughts on seasonable colours have led us too far into autumn and we must retrace our steps. Until the frosts wreak their final havoc, flowers in the garden have an illusion of summer; roses can bloom almost as profusely in September as they do in June, and only stems and leaves have lost their initial shining brilliance, more aware perhaps than the flowers themselves of the fading year. Zinnias, although less vivid, are still a most useful addition to our arrangements. Tritomas and montbretias provide the points and spikes which are difficult to find when gladioli end, and crinums give way to 'Belladonna' lilies which have the same texture and formation although not the same range of colour.

Nerines are less well known as garden flowers, although they are familiar enough in the shops at this time. They have a delicacy among the heavier autumn flowers which is invaluable, and come in shades of scarlet, clear bright pink and also, more recently, whites and flames. The hardier varieties are not difficult to grow provided they are given a sheltered spot and protection from severe frost.

Hydrangeas now are tinged with green, and as they change in tone, can be picked for drying. I have huge bowls of mixed hydrangeas all over the house at this time of year, as I find that they dry best if initially placed in water. (See Chapter 7.) Not only are they most decorative if arranged on their own, but the heads remain unblemished when allowed space in which to dry, and the leaves can be removed as they fade.

Although dahlias come into flower during the months of summer, they are nevertheless truly part of the autumn scene. They offer us every colour imaginable, other than blue, and carry their clear brilliance undimmed until cut down by the first frost. In colour, shape and varied texture they are lovely things, so let us enjoy them while we may. Unfortunately they are not very long-lasting, particularly if bought from a shop; but if gathered in a garden, they can retain their beauty for several days. It is necessary to remove all the leaves that could lie beneath the water-level, as these go brown and slimy in a matter of hours and foul the water. Nor will dahlias last well if picked while wet. They are charming arranged by themselves, as those with slender stems are adaptable to any design. In mixed groups they should be placed where they can be easily renewed, as in all probability they will not last as long as their companions.

What would we do without chrysanthemums, so aptly called 'our gallant garden mums'? The ravages of frost, fatal to dahlias and geraniums, can leave chrysanthemums untouched and gaily blooming, and, with the minimum of protection, they will last far into the winter. Flat or rounded, huge or small, they are one of the most useful and popular of flowers. Together with the spray variety, they are now available almost throughout the year in a range of colours which can harmonize with any scheme. The Rayonnantes and lovely singles, as yet more seasonably restricted to the autumn and winter months, offer us flowers of great elegance and a delicacy of form not normally associated with the stalwart chrysanthemum. All varieties have tremendously long-lasting qualities, generally far beyond the life of their leaves. It is best, therefore, to remove the lower ones and to strip off the remainder as they fade. The heads of all varieties of chrysanthemums need protection, as a bump or a bang, even when packed, can cause the petals to shatter and the heads to disintegrate. In company with all woody-stemmed flowers they require their stems to be split or hammered, followed by a long drink in warm water before being arranged.

The large-headed chrysanthemums are not easy flowers to arrange, particularly by themselves. So often we are in possession of no more than half a dozen and it is difficult to decide how to use them to best advantage. I think they should be considered in proportion to their setting, instead of numerically, and placed against a background big enough for their dimensions. For this purpose, as we obviously do not want a mountainous arrangement, the necessary effect can be achieved by a light shadowy outline made with such material as ferns or bracken with seed-heads, either dried or fresh. Brown larch branches, gaily bedecked with their tiny cones, or lichen-covered branches are equally suitable, as they give an illusion of size without heaviness.

Lichen is a type of alga and fungus together which grows very considerably in woodlands in Scotland and Cornwall and also, of course, though to a lesser degree, in damp woods and on rocks everywhere. The branches and twigs so covered are extremely brittle and cannot be packed easily. On many Cornish holidays I have, together with my understandably complaining family, been forced to send luggage home by train while the precious branches filled the car to the roof and necessitated cramped quarters and acute discomfort for the unfortunate travellers. For me, at least, the effort has been worth while, as the branches, with their delicate lace-like overlay in all shades of silvery grey to green, are outstanding by themselves or as an outline for many autumn or winter flowers. Try them with pale bronze chrysanthemums, green seed-heads of hemlock, and perhaps a few burnished copper-coloured bergenia leaves. Or, when the single chrysanthemums appear, the white 'Surfside' or the fragile shell-pink 'Venoya' are uniquely lovely alone with grey lichen, as are the heads of hydrangea when they turn in autumn to the most subtle sea-green shades, tinged with mauves and purples and faded rose. As the branches are too brittle to be coaxed into any shape other than those they bear naturally, it is wisest to choose stems that suit some particular vase and to let the flowers follow the lines taken, however weird they may appear at times. Pewter and bronze are a good foil for lichen, and I have a bronze Persian wine jug which shows off the occasionally weird-shaped branches to perfection.

Berries

At this time of year berries take precedence over many flowers and foliages, and can be as lovely on their own as when they are used with other material. Unfortunately the leaves of many deciduous shrubs are blemished by the time the berries reach perfection, and it is, therefore, necessary to remove most, and sometimes all, of them. These varieties are not attractive on their own, as the stripped branches have an alarmed, undressed look and are better among the softness of flowers and other leaves. Berries that are beautiful on their own, provided dead wood and any damaged leaves are removed, are such types as snowberries (*Symphoricarpus*), pink and white pernettyas, crimson skimmias, orange rowans and most of the prickly berberises, though, as with roses, it is advisable to dethorn at least part of the stems before attempting to arrange them.

Between pages 88 and 89 is an illustration showing two heavily berried branches of *Berberis* 'Sibbertoft Coral' spilling out of the narrow neck of a Persian wine jug. The natural fall of these decorative stems required few artifices in the manner of their arrangement except to incline one of them gently in line with the spout.

Alternatively, berries with fruit and leaves, arranged either on a flat dish or

FIGURE 24

a stemmed china cake-stand, can be a welcome change when flowers are scarce and expensive. Although some stems will require water, the fruit can lie on top of slightly raised wire-netting or, where the dish is big enough, a separate bowl can rest in the middle and be adequately hidden by the fruit arranged at its base. Try snowberries arranged with green and white gourds, grasses and variegated ivies; pink pernettya berries, aubergines, purple grapes or blackberries with leaves of mauve *Begonia rex*; or the crimson leaves and translucent red berries of the native guelder rose with scarlet peppers, striped croton leaves and trails of red vine. (See Figure 24 for position of a separate vase on a flat dish.)

Autumn leaves

I thought I knew about the colours of changing leaves until one autumn when I had occasion to fly to Canada and was able to spend a never-to-be-forgotten day in the Laurentian mountains north of Montreal. For a week or so each year the mountain sides are clothed in a medley of colour that beggars all description, and it was my good fortune to be there at exactly the right time. Led by the maples, the trees change rapidly with the first frost to a multitudinous array of lime and saffron yellow, monochromes of gold and the whole gamut of red, shading from pale salmon-pink through coral, flame and mulberry, to burnished mahogany brown. Silhouetted against this blazing background, the dark pines and silvery boles of the birch trees stand as sentinels. To attempt description of this scenic conflagration is, of course, useless and presumptuous, but to remind me of a splendour that could soon become unreal I brought back, pressed between newspapers in my limited luggage, a selection of gathered leaves which still glow in a beauty I had not seen before. For me they emphasize the fact that nothing we can do with flowers and foliage can dim Nature's own fantastic palette. So let us be bold with autumn colours and depict in our arrangements the dying year's flamboyant gesture to the end of growth.

It is well to remember that brilliance can rarely be achieved successfuly with one tone only, and that tawny autumn colours need pinks and flames and glowing scarlets to reproduce the richness we associate with fruits and berries. Try the following arrangement and see how the conflicting shades combine to a pleasing whole. For background a few stems of autumnal-tinted leaves such as red oak, azalea or peony foliage, with yellowing blades of montbretia for the tallest point. About six stems of spray chrysanthemums to fill in the outline, of which the amber-coloured 'Gaiety' would be a good choice; a similar amount of flame and scarlet dahlias for the centre and a few stems of coral red 'Montesuma' roses for a focal point. Autumn groups are nearly always improved by the addition of berries, and euonymus (spindle-berry) would be suitable here as the pinkish berries would link the reddening foliage with the brilliant roses.

Preserved leaves are useful through the autumn and winter months, though we must be careful not to fall into the error of leaving them unattended too long in the assumption that they can be a perpetual decoration. Like furniture, they need occasional dusting and moving around, and are of more value if arranged with a few fresh flowers. Beech leaves preserve well and should be picked before they turn colour. Opinions differ as to the amount of glycerine required, but I have found equal parts of glycerine and water satisfactory, and there should be sufficient to cover the stems to a depth of several inches. Hydrangeas can also be preserved, and so in fact can many other things, provided we like the pale brown tone most of them assume when the glycerine is absorbed. Although this shade is quite attractive in autumn and winter groups it has its limitations, and I prefer the shining dark green of evergreens of which there is such a choice available.

Purposely I have mentioned few of these, as I feel we should keep them for decoration during the winter months when the garden is finally at an end and all the remnants of summer and autumn foliages have become rusty-leaved and tattered.

House plants

I think the vogue for house plants as decorations in our homes is having a detrimental effect on preserved or dried material; and, perhaps, rightly so. Although the initial cost may be a little high, a bowl of living plants will last for weeks, or even months, and growing as they do before our eyes they supply perpetual interest as well as a most elegant decoration. Many are lovely by themselves and many are suitable for grouping, as in an arrangement of gathered flowers. Those of erect growth with shiny leathery leaves—such as the rubber plants, the handsome Monsteras and the San-sevierias—are completely at home in large-windowed modern rooms. They have tremendously long-lasting qualities and seem impervious to the effects of central heating which spells death to so many plants and flowers. As with evergreens, their leaves need dusting and an occasional polishing with a damp or oily cloth and, of course, attention to their drinking requirements. Once a plant has died from lack of water, no amount of replenishment will bring it back to life again.

Ferns, and the immense variety of variegated ivies and tradescantias, are invaluable for decoration owing to their graceful trailing habit of growth. There is a delicious pale pink tradescantia, initially shown by Rochfords, that I long to own in great quantities. These trailing plants need more attention than the foregoing, both in the amount of water they require and the occasional removal of spent leaves. Particularly they enjoy a gentle spraying, and ferns will last for months if their fronds as well as their roots receive water.

Owing to their great variety of colour, size and texture, *Begonia rex* leaves are both a unique decoration by themselves and a salient feature in a mixed arrangement. I have beside me now, in November, a colourful bowl of mixed plants which look as healthy as when they were potted up two months ago. The bowl is wide-lipped, on a short stem, which permits the trailing plants to cascade gracefully over the rim. An upright plant of croton leaves supplies the height, with *Hedera helix* 'Chicago' on one side and pink-tinged hoya on the other. The necessary softness is given by a Cocos palm, and a beautifully coloured and shaded *Begonia rex* makes the centre. The plants were firmed in with peat, which can be bought in Cellophane bags at most florists, and any gaps were moss-covered.

If you have been spell-bound, as I have, by Rochford's lovely stand at the annual Chelsea Flower Show, you will want to know more about the types and care of these plants which have become so popular for decoration. *The Rochford Book of House Plants* is a mine of information on a subject that can be bewildering for the uninitiated, and simplifies the choice of what can be suitable for your own particular requirements.

The Jardinière

Care should be taken over the containers into which we put these plants. Too often we see a lovely plant, still in its utilitarian flower-pot, standing disconsolately on a kitchen saucer; and not even a carefully chosen saucer but one that has long since lost its cup and is useless for any other purpose. To my mind this is on a par with putting roses in a jam-jar and shows neither respect nor consideration for an object of beauty.

The proper exploitation of this increasingly popular medium for the decoration of our homes deserves the same enthusiasm that sends us hot-foot in search of the perfect vase to hold some cherished flowers. It should not be difficult to find something suitable. The *Jardinière* dates back to the last century and the dictionary lists the word as 'ornamental pot or stand for the display of growing flowers'. Through the years we have come to associate the word with a plant table, rather than a single container, but there must be many pieces of old china which were designed to hold flower-pots of various sizes. Modern pottery also offers us charming designs to meet this revival, and against a contemporary background a single plant of bold leaves rising from a tube-like jar of Scandinavian pottery immediately becomes part of the décor. In old houses, where there is gleaming oak or dark panelling, copper preserving-pans make excellent containers provided they are kept well polished. Wine-coolers and *Jardinière* tables, already conveniently metal-lined, are best of all for a large number of plants, and Victorian wrought-iron plant tables, although originally in-

Orchids for decoration in a dolphin lustre vase. Minute *Aranda*
orchids with tradescantia are on one side with brown grasses on the
other while the centre is filled in with four pinkish-brown orchids of
a *Vanda* hybrid called 'Tan Chan Yau'. A small group such as this
will last for weeks.

Above: A single stem of pure white *Phalaenopsis* orchids in a bud vase.
Right: Two heavily berried branches of *Berberis* 'Sibbertoft Coral' in a Persian wine jug.

House plants and flowers in an elegant *Jardinière*. Two varieties of the genus *Dracaena* below a spectacular Bromeliad on the left with trails of variegated ivy, *Hedera helix* 'Glacier', on the right. Pink camellias and 'May Time' tulips were added to lend colour among these dramatic leaves.

tended for the garden, are equally at home indoors. Much of the modern wrought-iron is well-designed for this purpose also, and I have found stands in bamboo which make a perfect setting for plants. Containers can also be made from painted cake- or biscuit-tins; or oblong tins can be covered with bark or driftwood to make attractive troughs. In fact, the search for the suitable *Jardinière* can be as rewarding as that for the perfect vase. Anything that can contribute to the general scheme of decoration will naturally enhance the display of these lovely house plants which are now so easily available to us all. And there is really no excuse at all for the saucer.

Orchids

I would like to end this chapter with a word about a flower not normally associated with decoration. For years I had a slight prejudice against orchids. They had their place, I felt, in floristry, but owing to their price and way of growth I did not consider their potentialities in the field of flower arrangement.

The small, round *Odontoglossum* has always been a delicately pretty flower, and also an exorbitantly expensive one; but the traditional heavy-lipped, three-cornered orchid, such as a *Cattleya*, is difficult to use in most circumstances and held for me little charm. But now, each year, new varieties become available as growers increase their knowledge about this strange tropical flower. Because of my early prejudice I foolishly averted my eyes from their increasing beauty and refused to be beguiled, thereby depriving myself too long of a unique delight. Orchids do not look like orchids any more. More often they look like butterflies poised for flight. A bride's bouquet made entirely of pure white *Phalaenopsis* orchids can be the most ethereal thing imaginable. But that, of course, has nothing to do with this chapter. What is relevant is that many varieties of orchids can be brought here by air from Malaya and other places to sell at a reasonable price at a time when our own flowers are becoming scarce and expensive. Orchids will last for weeks, with no loss of colour or signs of fading, and then it is no extravagance to use them for a small arrangement. It has always been difficult to find a companion flower for orchids as they are essentially a type unto themselves. This problem is now eased by the comparatively low cost of long delicate stems of minute spider *Aranda orchids*, which soften the outline for the bigger varieties. The little dolphin lustre vase, illustrated facing page 88, is an example of this. A stem of golden brown *Aranda* 'Deborah' with tradescantia is on one side, with brown grasses on the other. Four pinkish-brown round orchids of a *Vanda* hybrid called 'Tan Chan Yau' filled in the centre, and the whole made a tiny autumnal-coloured group that maintained its beauty for weeks. In complete contrast is the illustration between pages 88 and 89, where a single stem of pure white *Phalaenopsis* orchids displays its perfection alone in a white bud vase. I remember, on one extravagant occasion, arranging stems of white, brown-flecked *Odontoglossum* orchids together with lace-like cow parsley (the seed-heads could have almost the same effect), and these oddly assorted, but completely harmonious, companions spilled out of a gilt and crystal 'compotier' on to a dinner-table covered with a buff-coloured silk organza cloth.

Perhaps, some day, orchids will become reasonable enough in price for us to use them with the abandon we ascribe to flowers of more fleeting characteristics. Until then, let us enjoy them occasionally during the weeks of autumn when delicate flowers are hard to come by, and learn to know them in their natural state rather than as beheaded flowers for use only in floristry. As I have done, you too will probably fall under their spell.

7. Green Groups in Winter

Although winter may seem to many of us to be the longest season of all, it is, in fact, surprisingly short where flowers are concerned. A mild autumn will enable many flowers to linger on despite the fact that growth has ended. Even when frosts have put an end to everything vulnerable, the hardy chrysanthemums and late roses will be found still blooming in sheltered places far into November.

It is, I think, desirable to follow the rhythm of the seasons by using the quiet colours that would naturally be found outside during the early weeks of winter and, in contrast to the richness we have enjoyed in autumn, the greys and browns of seed-heads, the sea-greens and peacock-blue tones of fading hydrangeas, the shining dark leaves of evergreens and the natural tawny colours of chrysanthemums are more satisfying at this time than all the splendour of hot-house flowers. It is not, after all, for long that we need restrict ourselves to these less colourful shades, as the glittering nonsense of Christmas decorations invades our homes and public places by mid-December and, when these have served their purpose, the shops are filled with bright spring flowers so that a return to the faded tones of November and December would be impossible.

As it is expensive to buy early spring flowers continually, and the life of forced flowers is not very long, this is the moment, therefore, when brilliant colour can be introduced by growing plants; a *Jardinière* table, or large flat bowl, filled with colourful bulb flowers and green plants will last for weeks and span the gap between the quiet tones of winter and the clear brilliance that comes with spring. And then, at all times, there are evergreens which, when arranged attractively and kept clean and polished, are wholly satisfying as decorations throughout the winter months.

The dried group

As I have said, I think the vogue for house plants as decoration is taking the place of preserved or dried material. Despite this fact there is, nevertheless, a time when seed-heads, dried ferns and fading flowers have their rightful place in flower arrangement either as a background for a few fresh flowers or as an arrangement on their own. During those weeks between the end of growth and Christmas they seem eminently suitable for decoration, as they are typical of the bare winter scene in their pale, obscure colours and leafless stems. But, to my mind, they are not suitable for this purpose when they are resuscitated, limp and rather dusty, to fill the gaps left by the removal of Christmas decorations. It is, admittedly, a lot of trouble to dry and preserve such material for use over only a short period, but the same can surely be said of the cultivation and preparation of all things necessary for flower arrangement whatever the season. In its rightful place dried material can be a most lovely and adequate decoration at a time when fresh flowers are scarce and also inordinately expensive.

Facing page 96 is an illustration of a dried arrangement, the main feature of which is the collection of maple leaves I had brought back, dried and pressed, from Canada. In view of their incredible colour, the deeper tones of which were ruby red and mulberry, I was at a loss to find a suitable vase. It was found, eventually, on a friend's mantelpiece and was one of a pair of garnet-coloured glass chalices, originally hung with lustres but from which the lustres had long since disappeared. It was obligingly loaned for the occasion, and immediately the colours fell into place like a carefully designed mosaic. I used for my highest point two brown seed-heads of verbascum, one in front of the other, and these were flanked on one side by a yellowing montbretia leaf and on the other by pale, pinkish buff maize. Further montbretia leaves were inserted horizontally to form the long side arms, and drifts of maple leaves, ranging in colour from faded saffron through all shades of coral red to dark mahogany brown, were placed centrally and to the sides to complete the shape. The maple leaves had, of course, no stems, and so were wired on to false stems as described in Chapter 2, Figure 21, and were then made into sprays of three leaves. Dried bracken filled in the outline, while some dried fern, which still retained its original clear green, spilled out in front. Two heads of globe artichokes, with shining outside petals, formed the heart, with the dried head of the flower of an *Aechmea rhodocyanea* (one of Rochford's most spectacular house plants) immediately above them. Grey alliums, dark ruby-red seed-heads of *Sedum maximum atropurpureum* and almost metallic-hued blue hydrangeas completed a group that was as colourful as many a one of fresh flowers and yet, over all, was typical of the naturally fading colours of any winter scene. Placed against a background of sea-green panelling with near-by curtains of similar colour, it seemed completely complementary to its surroundings. In arrangements of this kind it is advisable to weight the vase with either a metal pin-holder, a few pebbles or a little sand.

It is particularly important that there should be no overcrowding with dried arrangements, so that the skeleton material stands out in all its delicate tracery. On those occasions when it is used in conjunction with fresh flowers, it is preferable, I think, to use it as a background and to let the flowers become the main feature of the arrangement. The vase should then be filled with water and the arrangement re-done when necessary, even though the dried material can be used repeatedly. If, on the other hand, the material is to be stored or used again in a wholly dried group, the stems should be wiped dry with a clean cloth.

The method of drying material for this purpose varies, as some types should be pressed flat, some hung head down to dry, while others retain their colours better if, when stripped of leaves, they are placed initially in a little water. The following suggestions are an indication of the vast variety of suitable material which is available in every garden and hedgerow for those with discerning eyes and—perhaps more important—sufficient patience to gather and harvest the necessary material throughout the summer and autumn for use during the lean months of winter.

Before setting out to collect any material at all, it is advisable, however, to make a plan of what will be required. In just the same way as flowers and foliages would be gathered for an arrangement of fresh flowers, so it should be remembered that pointed and light-textured material will be necessary for the outline and background, and that more solid pieces are required for the central and focal points. As a dried arrangement can easily look rather desiccated and is inevitably lustreless, some high-lights will be

93

necessary in the shape of very pale material, while the contrast of really dark colours is also beneficial.

Suitable material for backgrounds

All types of fern and bracken are useful. The former, including osmunda, can be picked while still green, but this royal fern can also be dried when it has turned a golden tan, although it should be cut well before it has started to curl at the edges. Similarly, bracken should have turned in colour but should still be pliable. The blade-like leaves of the giant montbretias, those of many gladioli, the fallen brown leaves of *Magnolia grandiflora* and the great leaves of the Himalayan rhododendron all press well and offer a variety of form and texture for the backing of dried arrangements. All these should be laid out flat (and separately) between newspapers, which are then placed beneath rugs or carpets for a few weeks. Care must be taken when these are stored, as many become brittle (see page 86). It is wisest to pack them flat, between newspapers, pending their use in decorations.

The 'skeletonized' leaves of *Magnolia grandiflora* and bleached *Adiantum* are now commercially prepared and are procurable from most good florists during the weeks before Christmas. Their biscuit-coloured transparency is an attractive contrast to many of the darker and more solid types of dried material, and both are of great value in Christmas decorations. The 'skeletonized' leaves are, of course, without stems, but can be wired on to twigs or branches or given false stems as described in Chapter 2, Figure 21. Certain leafless branches such as lichen-covered branches, larch branches covered in tiny brown fir-cones and stems of Hornbeam, with their pendant 'keys', also make good outlines for dried arrangements.

Seed-heads generally dry quite well if hung head down in separate varieties in a cool, dry place. Among those suitable for backgrounds are delphiniums, verbascums, foxgloves, poppies and many lilies, maize and the rather weird-shaped bracts of acanthus and onopordon. Ornamental and hedgerow grasses are also effective if kept bunched together when dried.

Suitable material for central and focal points

Hydrangeas, which are perhaps the most useful of all for this purpose, should not be picked until they begin to change in colour, at which time they can be gathered, stripped of leaves and placed in an inch or two of water until all moisture is absorbed. This prevents them becoming too brittle and also helps to retain the lovely subtle colours. If space permits they are best left untouched (and are, incidentally, immensely decorative), but if they must be moved they should be loosely tied together and hung head down in a dry place or, alternatively, packed in open boxes until required. The dried flowers of artichokes and yarrow, seed-heads of alliums, agapanthus and alstroemerias all make rounded heads which are so necessary for the centres of any arrangement, and, from the hedge-rows, seed-heads of hemlock and wild fennel are equally useful.

Material suitable for trails

Clematis, which forms a seed-head of spidery tendrils similar to 'Old Man's Beard', is extremely useful. The green amaranthus and trails of hops also dry quite well when stripped of leaves, but are apt to turn beige-coloured. 'Old Man's Beard' itself can be given the glycerine treatment and will last longer without becoming brittle.

Green groups

From autumn until spring, evergreens play an important part in decorations either as a background for hot-house flowers or as an entirely green arrangement. A very few flowers will show to far greater advantage if the design of the arrangement is both outlined, and largely filled in, with suitable evergreens before the insertion of any flowers at all.

Unfortunately, to many, the thought of evergreens conjures up pictures of laurel and privet, rhododendrons and pittosporum which, though suitable enough in the right place, could not constitute a basis for attractive or unusual groups. When colour has gone, form becomes even more important and a well-chosen arrangement of winter evergreens should be as light in outline and as graceful in design as any collection of flowers. The long-lasting grey-leaved eucalyptus is available in the shops throughout the winter and adds grace and charm to any arrangement. It has a number of varieties, from the more common round-leaved forms to the exotic *Eucalyptus globulus* whose cream or grey-blue buds open finally into tasselled flowers.

THE DRIED GROUP

It is not always necessary to dry material too meticulously for use in these arrangements, as many plants will dry naturally on the root if we can shut our eyes to some temporary untidiness in the border. Indeed, a wealth of treaures can be found among the stems of herbaceous plants if these are left to fade as nature intended and are not cut down immediately the flowering period ends.

The group shown here illustrates both types of material. The ferns, bracken, maple and montbretia leaves were, of course, dried and pressed between newspapers for a week or so prior to use, as otherwise they would have shrivelled and had little value in decoration. On the other hand, the brown seed-heads of verbascum, which form the spine, the buff-coloured maize on the left with, just below it, the blood-red seed-heads of *Sedum maximum atropurpureum* were all picked from the garden and used directly in the arrangement. This particular variety of sedum is a most useful perennial, as the deep-red leaves and stems are effective among clashing red flowers and they also keep their colour remarkably well in dried arrangements.

On this occasion the artichoke and allium heads were also picked from the plant, by which time the former had lost their purple tinge and turned pale brown but the latter were grey and still had a softness in their heads. Alliums will, unfortunately, disintegrate entirely if left on the root too long. The pinkish flower in the centre is an *Aechmea rhodocyanea* which was also left to dry on the root (in this case of a spectacular house plant), but the hydrangea heads were dried differently. I find that these most useful of all flower-heads for winter arrangements retain their colour best if placed initially in an inch or two of water and are dried in a warm dry atmosphere. The moment for picking is, of course, also all-important as the heads will not dry if the petals are still soft. They should feel papery to the touch and be turning in colour from pink or white to green or from blue to metallic hues. The placing of stems in shallow water initially also applies to other flower-heads, such as achilleas, as it helps to retain the colour.

SINGLE CHRYSANTHEMUMS WITH WINTER FOLIAGE

The pale winter sun shines here on these lovely apricot-coloured chrysanthemums called 'Valencia' and is reflected again in the gilded cherub vase and the silvery-gold leaves of *Elaeagnus glabra*. This variety of elaeagnus comes to me from Cornwall during the winter months and is valuable in that the rambling stems are long enough to outline even large arrangements while the metallic lustre on the underside of the leaves gives a brilliance which is rare among evergreen foliages.

Chrysanthemums are often thought to be difficult flowers to arrange because they can be stiff-stemmed and rather heavy-headed, but this generally applies only to the large specimen blooms and there are vast numbers among the smaller varieties which have stems flexible enough to be adaptable to any design. Single chrysanthemums, such as those shown here, are to me quite exquisite and have the elegance of single peonies with the advantage of long-lasting qualities. They are, however, even more expensive than others of their genus, so it is advisable to display them against a background of suitable foliage which, in this case, is supplied by the elaeagnus and cream-budded sprays of *Eucalyptus globulus*. This is useful among large-headed flowers as it has a softening quality similar to that given by sprays of berries.

The deeply serrated artichoke leaves give an appearance of strength to this fountain-shaped design, and it can be seen that they stem from a central source, two being flung upward and backward for balance while the other two flow forward and downward to emphasize the cascading effect.

The gilded fruit bowl, supported by the figure of a cherub, is one of my most useful containers as it lends itself to a variety of arrangements. The wide-lipped vessel can contain thick-stemmed plants (such as the artichoke leaves) or, on occasions, the roots of plants themselves. This is helpful when such leaves as coleus are required, as these rarely last when cut, or when hydrangea is used while still immature. This type of vase also makes a perfect base for cones of fruit and flowers.

I grow the hardy *Eucalyptus gunnii* in my garden and, because the tree is still young, the slender stems pass through the centre of the almost circular leaves in the manner of pennies threaded on a string. Later on the leaves become elongated and are alternated on the stems, but, meanwhile, a single branch of this immature growth will produce stems which are erect, curving or bunched together from a single point so that the shorter pieces will cascade like falling stars, and a whole arrangement can be built up from this foliage alone. The young growth on several species of eucalyptus has the same rounded or heart-shaped leaves which later become longer, narrower and greener.

Grevillea foliage is more pointed in form and has narrow leaves which are silver backed. It, too, is available in the shops throughout most of the winter.

For those with gardens there are a variety of evergreens which are not difficult to grow and which add immeasurably to the scope of arrangements in winter-time. Among the easiest to grow, and the most useful to pick, are the mahonias, the leaves of which shine as though polished, and some varieties turn a burnished red-bronze in winter. Most species bear arching racemes of yellow flowers in early spring which are deliciously scented. Less well known, but of great value in winter decoration, is variegated elaeagnus, *Elaeagnus pungens* 'Maculata' (generally sold as *E. pungens* 'Aureo-variegata'), which has bright yellow-patterned leaves edged in dark green. *Elaeagnus glabra* develops long wands covered with silvery-gold backed leaves and is a most elegant addition to almost any winter group. The evergreen shrubs of *Pieris japonica* (Andromeda) should not be forgotten. In sheltered gardens the tiny white flowers blossom in early spring, but long before that time a single stem which contains a spray of pinkish buds will lighten a green arrangement in a way that nothing else will do.

Most gardens of any age will probably possess some of the following shrubs, any of which will add substance to a green arrangement. Golden or variegated privet, dark green myrtle, laurustinus (generally rather unjustly disregarded) with clusters of pink buds which blossom in winter into white flowers, the abundant foliage of the common ponticum rhododendrum, the bright green skimmias and the huge shining leaves of *Magnolia grandiflora*. Laurel, too, is excellent if it is fresh and green and highly polished, and its variegated form, *Aucuba japonica* 'Variegata', is also useful. Many types of cupressus, both of the green and grey varieties, are good additions to winter groups but are, on the whole, better with other evergreens than with flowers. The points that are necessary for many outlines can be found in yucca leaves or those of *Phormium tenax*, or with bare sprays of broom. And for all the trails that are so necessary for grace there is the common ivy—the firm-stemmed type that grows up walls and trees. It will need prising off with a knife, but it will keep its line indefinitely and will repay the trouble taken in its gathering.

I have left camellia foliage to the end as its beauty should generally be left to stand alone. It is uniquely beautiful as a single-stem decoration or in a massed arrangement on its own, but, equally, a few stems will add form and grace to any mixed arrangement.

The disadvantage with evergreens, however, is that even those found in the country are dirty and require careful cleaning before being used for decoration. All large-leaved foliages (and this includes camellia) should have each leaf polished with a damp rag, and small-leaved bushy foliage should either be rinsed under a tap, or well sprayed, to remove dust and dirt. Damaged or imperfect leaves must be removed, as well as any dead wood, and some pruning may be necessary to eliminate off-shoots when their leaves would face the wrong way, or where they would make the outline branches too heavy. Although an evergreen arrangement will probably last considerably longer than any other type of fresh material, it should not be regarded as a perpetual decoration as its charm remains only so long as it is alive and shiningly healthy. Evergreens are also avid drinkers, and vases containing them need constant attention and replenishment. Some useful mixtures could be:

Myrtle and ivy for the background and trailing side pieces, suitably pruned rhododendron for the centre and some stems of *Pieris japonica* or mahonia for a focal point.

Golden privet with variegated elaeagnus to frame a cluster of the great, pale green leaves of *Magnolia grandiflora* or *Aucuba japonica* 'Variegata'.

A silvery-grey mixture of grevillea with various eucalyptus foliage and some stems of silver cupresses, such as *C. arizonica* to give solidity or, alternatively, a head or two of *Euphorbia wulfenii* which remains evergreen through the winter.

Evergreens with winter flowers

The photograph facing page 97 illustrates the manner in which a few flowers can be made to look more by the addition of suitable foliages. A dozen fragile, apricot-coloured single chrysanthemums called 'Valencia' were arranged with a few stems of *Elaeagnus glabra*, cream-budded *Eucalyptus globulus* and the last four artichoke leaves to escape the winter frosts. The graceful stems of both foliages provided the necessary outline for the fountain-shaped design, and the silvery-gold leaves of the elaeagnus repeated the shimmering gilt of the Italian fruit bowl in which the group was arranged. The sweeping lines of the artichoke leaves gave the necessary strength to the centre and to the upward and back-flung main stems, so that the design was complete before the insertion of a single flower. Set against a Flemish tapestry screen the whole arrangement glowed with the pale warmth of winter sunlight and retained its beauty for more than a week during one dark December.

Similar arrangements could be made with a number of other types of foliages and flowers, among which hot-house carnations would be particularly suitable for this type of design as their stems are gracefully flexible. They are not an extravagance at this time of year, as they will last for a week at least with careful treatment and their range of colour suits all tastes.

Hot-house flowers

Wise expenditure on winter flowers is a matter for thought and consideration. Too often we restrict ourselves to chrysanthemums only because of their well-known durability, but there are many varieties of flowers which will last almost as well if given the correct treatment.

I have mentioned nerines in the chapter on autumn flowers, but these delicate leafless flowers remain in the shops until after Christmas and their clear colours and fragile umbels of flower-heads make them suitable companions for the heavier chrysanthemums. Later on, the fleshy-stemmed echeverias are a wise purchase, as they will last for weeks and their coral-tinted leaves and buds blend with both pink or flame arrangements.

Euphorbia fulgens is another good buy (though an expensive one), as the long pendant stems, closely covered in narrow dark leaves and star-like orange flowers, are gracefully effective. They last better if the tips of the stems are burned or 'boiled', as euphobias are all of the 'bleeding' variety. This also, of course, applies to poinsettias, which become available at this time and make a spectacular splash of colour in a winter arrangement. There are now pink and white varieties as well as red.

As long as they are available, the tiny roses, pink 'Carol' and red 'Garnet', are worth buying as their long-lasting qualities repay their initial cost.

The former is shown arranged with hot-house-grown lily of the valley in the illustration facing page 104. This was photographed in November and, at a time when sweetly-scented flowers are rare, this little group would have great charm, especially as a present for someone who was ill. It may seem strangely out of season to have lily of the valley in the winter, but this lovely flower, like many others, is now almost perpetually available, chiefly, perhaps, because it is so popular for bride's bouquets. The stems and foliage are of a much paler green in the hot-house variety than in those of the garden type and are, in consequence, of great use in decoration. The iridescent colours of the mother-of-pearl shell were an added attraction and helped to eke out a small number of flowers.

The regal-looking Hippeastrum (more commonly known as 'amaryllis'), is to be found in the shops in November and continues until early spring. A stem or two is not an extravagance as these lily-like flowers will last for a week or so, and one stem alone is a dramatic decoration together with a bare branch in a tubular vase or as a focal point in groups of flame or red. The white, pink or striped varieties, although undeniably beautiful, are less dramatically effective.

The heart-shaped anthurium with its curious long tongue is, perhaps, more than any other plant the synthesis of all ideas of what constitutes an obvious hot-house flower. Its leaf is almost equally spectacular, and both are extremely long-lasting. Although the range of colour is incredible, and includes a unique clear pink, it is nevertheless a difficult flower to arrange, perhaps because of a lack of suitable companions. White anthuriums mingle satisfactorily among other white flowers, as their wax-like purity can be repeated in flowers around them, but the coloured ones often seem alien among others of their own shade. They are, I think, best used alone with their own dramatic leaves or, as this would prove inordinately expensive, as a central point in an arrangement of colourful mixed flowers. In a group of clashing reds they are particularly effective.

Flowers from the garden

The white Christmas rose (*Helleborus niger*), the bunches of green bells of the common hellebore (*H. foetidus*) and the delicately beautiful *Iris unguicularis* are the first flowers to be picked from the garden even before the turn of the year. The fragile looks of all belie their toughness, and even when brought indoors they have no objection to the dry warmth which is in such sharp contrast to the chill of their natural environment. All are long lasting, though the Christmas rose may need a rest in deep warm water in a cool place if the flowers show signs of becoming limp and soft. This exquisite flower should always find a place in our homes at Christmas time and, among the colourful glitter of artificial decorations, its purity is all the more outstanding. The soft clusters of little bells and starfish-shaped leaves of the common hellebore will last indefinitely if picked individually, but the main, shrubby stem is apt to go soft and may require re-cutting and further drinks in deep water. *Iris unguicularis* is best picked in bud to avoid damage to the delicate flowers.

House Plants

A *Jardinière* filled with growing plants is an effective decoration at all times, but never more so than during the weeks following Christmas when early spring flowers are frail and often leafless. Facing page 89 is an illustration of an elegant plant-table which contains a nucleus of green-house plants, among which pots of spring-flowering shrubs and flowers have been added. The house plants consisted of tall, striped leaves of a colourful Bromeliad on the left with a smaller *Dracaena sanderiana* drifting down in front of it. The mottled leaves of a rather different Dracaena plant called *D. godseffiana* 'Florida Beauty' formed the centre, and a Cocos fern and trails of 'Glacier' ivy were on the right. Among these lovely leaves were placed, on this occasion, a flowering camellia and some violet pointed tulips called 'May Time', but colour can be introduced by any flowers available and the changes rung as often as desired.

On the whole, house plants are best left in their own pots, which should be stood on a bed of small pebbles or clinkers, about an inch deep, in whatever container is chosen. The intervening spaces should be filled with peat (which retains moisture well) and the top covered with moss. Alternatively, they can be planted out in peaty soil, but it is then not so easy to change their positions or to introduce additional flowering shrubs or bulbs.

8. Flowers for Parties

Party decorations depend, to a certain extent, on an element of surprise. An arrangement which is sufficiently outstanding in beauty and originality to be a feature for comment adds considerably to the success of the occasion. Originality must, however, be tempered with suitability, as an unusual idea has no charm unless it is related to the background and to the occasion. It should, in fact, emphasize the reason for the gathering and, by the slight exaggeration of normality, add to the essential spirit of festivity and excitement which constitutes the perfect party.

Admittedly it is only on rare occasions that a theme can be carried out and original ideas translated into flowers, but the principle of suitability always applies as, for example, with table decorations; small baskets of gay flowers are entirely right on the supper tables for a young girl's dance, or for a luncheon party in the country, but would be out of place on any formal occasion. The type of decorations used in private houses are generally different from those suitable for hotels, while marquees—because of their size and impersonal appearance, due to lack of furnishings—lend themselves to variations in decoration which could not be employed elsewhere. When deciding upon a decoration for some special occasion, I think it is desirable, therefore, to consider, firstly the reason for the party and secondly any particular feature in the place to be decorated, and then to try to relate the two together by the type and colour scheme of the decorations.

In the following pages I will try to illustrate these points by giving examples of decorations which have proved successful in the past, and by offering suggestions for other arrangements which could be adjusted to the occasion and may provide a basis for further ideas to suit individual needs.

Pink 'Carol' roses and hot-house-grown lily of the valley were used
for this arrangement which was photographed in November. The
iridescent colours of the mother-of-pearl shell were an added
attraction.

Above: A table designed for the wedding cake. The rings of flowers could be placed round the tiers of the cake.

Right: A cloud of white sweet peas arranged in a silver bowl as a table decoration for a party.

Miniature cones are excellent decorations for small tables. Gardenias were used for this arrangement but roses, carnations and pinks are all suitable.

Table decorations

I think we should approach the subject of table decorations with a fairly open mind. Although it is usually considered that this type of arrangement should be kept low in order not to obscure the view of people sitting opposite each other, there are, nevertheless, many occasions when decorations of a different kind can be employed. Despite a prejudice to the contrary, tall arrangements are often most effective, especially on round tables or on long tables of adequate width. Decorated candelabras are always a noticeable feature and are easy to arrange in a number of ways. The illustration facing page 33 shows a three-branch candelabra which has been decorated with delicate pastel-coloured flowers, among which are two sprays of minute *Oncidium* orchids, blue leucocorynes (Glory of the Sun), *Jasminum polyanthum*, grape hyacinths, Lenten hellebores and a lovely single pink camellia. The flowers were arranged in small metal candle-cups, which are procurable at most florists, and were inserted into the candle-holders of the candelabra. When candles are used they should be placed in the cups before these are filled with wire-netting or Florapak, the latter being preferable for table decorations as it eliminates the risk of water spilling on table-cloths or polished surfaces. I find it simpler to crumble the Florapak into small pieces before soaking it in water, as it can then be firmly pressed down into the container to form a solid foundation for the reception of flower stems. But, even when Florapak is used, it is generally advisable to place one layer of wire-netting over the top of the container in order to prevent the crumbling and loosening of the Florapak. When the cups have been suitably prepared and inserted into the candle-holders, it is necessary to tie them to the candelabra with either silver wire or fuse wire, as there must be no risk of them tilting in any direction, especially if they are holding lighted candles as well as flowers.

Although the illustration described above shows a cascading design of flowers, there are many other ways of decorating candelabras which are equally effective, and single sticks of china, glass or silver can also be employed. Small flowers such as primroses, hardy cyclamens or gentians arranged in a solid ring, with leaves spread out around them to hide the metal cups, make an enchanting spring decoration, and similar solid rings of flowers can be done with small summer flowers such as cornflowers, candytuft, pinks or miniature roses, or the flowers can be combined with fruit like red cherries and tiny green grapes.

An alternative idea is to make moss rings to place round the base of the candelabras; these involve a measure of floristry but are most effective for a party where a number of tables containing candelabras require decoration. The 'broken' rings, the inside measurements of which should be just slightly larger than the base of the candelabra, are made by firmly binding a few handfuls of damp moss over a length of wire, cut to the correct length, until the width is about three-quarters of an inch, the ends being left unjoined to facilitate the fixture of the ring around the candelabra. A strip of polythene or cellophane should then be pinned to the underside to prevent any damage to the table surface. Small, long-lasting leaves, such as those of common or variegated ivy, are mounted in sprays on wire legs as described in Chapter 2 under 'Mounting flowers', and are inserted into the moss so that they cover the ring and reach table level on the outer side. Small flowers, similarly mounted, are also inserted in varying lengths to give a light and natural effect. The method described above is shown in Figures 25–27.

FIGURE 25   FIGURE 26   FIGURE 27

Cones, pyramids or domes of flowers make good table decorations because, despite their solidity, they are too neat to get in the way, neither do they obscure the view if kept in proper proportion to the table. They can be made in two ways, one of which is relatively simple, while the other involves floristry. Taking the latter first: Damp moss is pressed into a pyramidal or rounded shape and covered with two-inch wire-netting which should completely cover the base as well. The cone is then attached by wire

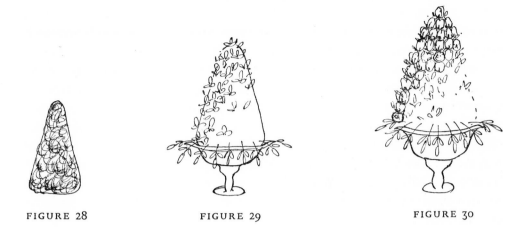

FIGURE 28   FIGURE 29   FIGURE 30

or string to the container, which, if it is light in weight, can be filled with a little damp sand. Suitable containers must, of course, be round and can be anything from a low bowl to a tall china, silver or gilt fruit bowl, but a stemmed container is always preferable. Miniature cones look charming in silver wine goblets and are excellent decorations for individual small tables.

The cone is first of all studded with small leaves which are pinned in place with short wires bent to form a hairpin. Roses, carnations, pinks—even, most extravagantly, gardenias as shown in the picture facing page 105—are all suitable for this type of work and are mounted as shown in Figure 20, Chapter 2, and then inserted in descending circles from the top. The final row is best done with sprays of leaves, which should be allowed to droop over the lip of the container in order to hide the wire that is holding the mossed cone in position. The necessary steps are shown in Figures 28–30. When completed, the cones should be lightly sprayed and covered with damp tissue paper until required.

The simpler method leaves the flowers in water, so that many varieties can be used which would not be suitable for floristry. For these cones the wire-netting is arranged to form a dome or pyramid three to four inches above the top of the container and is then firmly tied in place. The first few flowers, preferably smaller than the remainder, are inserted into the centre to form the highest point. Thereafter the flowers are inserted on shortening stems in increasing circles until the base is reached, ending, as before, with

107

a row of leaves. Care must be taken, however, to see that every stem reaches well below water-level and, as these have to be threaded through a larger amount of wire-netting than is usually the case, it is advisable to remove all leaves, thorns or broken-off shoots that might impede the way.

Table decorations vary according to the type of party concerned, but it is worth remembering that the table itself is the important feature and that it can, at night, be decorated regardless of its surroundings, which can be faded out by appropriate lighting. Flowers can be arranged in either of the ways described for all-round or oblong arrangements in Chapter 2 under 'Traditional designs', and nothing can be more lovely on a shining dark surface than clouds of white sweet peas arranged formally in a silver or crystal bowl, as shown in the illustration between pages 104 and 105, while roses of all colours are unsurpassed for these low arrangements as they lend themselves alike to simplicity or formality. On coloured tablecloths, or on unpolished or painted table-tops the rounded mound or flowers described in Chapter 2 under 'Flowers on their own' is often very effective, especially when the silver or china are of modern design. A wooden bowl of blazing marigolds on an ochre cloth, mixed red geraniums on natural unpolished wood, or a dome of brilliant pompon dahlias on a painted table-top have the strong impact of colour compatible with much modern décor.

I have rather mixed feelings about floating flower-heads in a shallow dish, which is a commonly-seen form of decoration. Given the right conditions certain flowers look charming when treated in this manner, but their horizontal position, and the cool effect of water, should appear to be their natural habitat rather than one that is super-imposed. Water-lilies, naturally, make a perfect decoration of this kind, and crystal or heavy glass make the best containers. As water-lilies are apt to close up, it is necessary to pick them when they are fully open and then either to force their petals gently backwards (which has the disadvantage of changing the shape of the flower) or to drop a little melted candle wax round the outer edge of the stamens which will keep the flowers pressed open.

The flowers of certain shrubs, notably camellias and some of the smaller type of rhododendrons, can look charming in a pool-like setting, especially when surrounded by a rosette of their own leaves. Gardenias, also, can be shown to advantage in this position, as the intricate manner in which their heavy crumpled petals lie folded one upon the other is clearly evident, and the glory of their scent adds considerably to the party feeling. It is, however, very difficult to define exactly why certain flowers look natural and others awkward when treated, in effect, like aquatic plants. Personally I avoid those that are borne on long and virtually leafless stems, and look for those that, in growth, lie amid well-formed leaves.

Parties in private houses

If the party is to be a luncheon, tea or dinner party where, for the most part, the guests will be sitting down, then I think that the decorations should be similar to those usually arranged in a house. Most hostesses have favourite positions for flowers, and there is no reason why these should be radically changed for a small and homely party. It is worth while, however, to give particular attention to the colour scheme so that any special feature in a room is accentuated, and for an evening party, when soft lights will be *de rigueur*, it is well to place a particularly lovely arrangement in some place where a lamp will shine down on it. On the other hand, if the occasion for the party is cocktails, a buffet meal, a reception or a dance, when the room will be crowded with people standing up, rather different principles apply. Decorations should be kept high, placed in salient positions, and be arranged in heavy vases so that even if down-flowing stems are touched there will be no fear of the vases tipping over.

The use of too many pedestal arrangements should be avoided in a private house and use could be made of suitable furniture on which to place flowers. One group on a pedestal is always a striking decoration in any big room but, if possible, the pedestal used should be in keeping with the furniture and not look as if it were part of a florist's equipment. A tall mantlepiece is a vantage-point, especially if there is a mirror above it and the whole mantle can advantageously be covered in flowers. A long tin trough is a useful container for this type of decoration as, to be effective, trails of foliage and flowers should be allowed to flow out to the end of the mantelpiece and to spill over the edge. I have a pair of chicken feeding-troughs, eighteen inches long by four and a half inches wide, which I have painted gold and which are invaluable, as they hold a lot of water (necessary above a fire) and are solid and heavy enough to take a large amount of flowers and foliage.

Niches or alcoves are safe and striking positions for flowers, particularly if spot-lit, while the top of any lovely cabinet or chest or marble-topped console table are all vantage-points on which to place a decoration. Although a grand piano is often considered to be a suitable place for flowers, I feel that as its primary use is for music it should be left unadorned unless, like so many in this radio-controlled age, it is a silent piece of inherited furniture.

A really dramatic arrangement in an entrance hall can set the tone for a party and make the guests eager and interested about what is to come. If the colour scheme permits, an arrangement of clashing red flowers is eye-catching and often controversial—who, after all, would think that orange, puce, pink and scarlet could mix happily together?—and can give people a subject for discussion while they are waiting to be received.

When valuable furniture is used as a stand for flower arrangements, great care should be taken to avoid any damage that might occur from water marks. Irreparable harm can be done to a beautifully polished or marquetry surface by the presence of even one unnoticed drop of water, and certain leaves have a tendency to syphon long after the decoration is completed. Although a glass mat or piece of thick felt cut to fit the base of the vase in use will give a measure of protection, it is sometimes advisable to cover the whole of a valuable surface with transparent material such as polythene or, preferably, the firmer perspex.

Parties in hotels

As hotels rarely have much furniture higher than table level it is generally advisable to place decorations on pedestals to gain the requisite height. The number of such arrangements is, of course, entirely dependent on the size and shape of the room, and the financial circumstances of the party giver, but the following suggestions may be helpful as a guide.

A long, narrow room will probably require a group at either end, with an arrangement on the buffet facing the entrance. A square room might require a large group at one end, where the host and hostess will receive their guests, one or two smaller groups facing the entrance and a decorated buffet at the far end. It is generally unnecessary to have decorations on the entrance side of the room. If the guests pass through a foyer, then this is the place for a spectacular arrangement, preferably in a different colour from the rest of the decorations. Tall mirrors make excellent backgrounds for flowers and, as in private houses, high mantelpieces are good vantage-points for decorations. Arrangements for the buffet table are best kept high, with the flowers well away from the table surfaces. Tall cones of roses or carnations or cones of fruit and flowers are not only striking as buffet decorations but they have the advantage of remaining intact throughout the party. Facing page 112 is an illustration of a mossed cone covered with 'Ophelia' roses, striped croton leaves, autumn berries, bunches of small grapes, echeverias and narrow leaves of *Chlorophytum* which was sumptuous enough for the grandest banquet and yet gay enough for an informal buffet party.

Parties in marquees

Decorations for marquees have to be planned with a map which, more often than not, bears little resemblance to the final erection. It is always advisable, therefore, to see the marquee as soon as it is up, as previously-laid plans may have to be radically altered. A marquee is, on the whole, an empty and rather characterless place which can be transformed with flowers, with ample scope for originality and gay ideas. First consideration, however, should be given to any existing features which may be enclosed within its walls, as these should be accentuated rather than ignored. I remember only too well the unfortunate occasion when a specially chosen colour scheme of apricot and flame was destroyed overnight by the unexpected blooming of a magnificent 'Michele Meilland' rose tree which covered the entire house wall enclosed within the marquee. This was probably caused by the sudden extra warmth from the marquee, but it was a factor which should have been considered in my calculations. Similarly, this can happen in reverse, as a colour scheme planned to match growing flowers or shrubs can come to naught when, perversely, these fail to flower at a given time. All the same, any outstanding feature should be emphasized and on page 114 I have given an example.

A CONE OF FRUIT AND FLOWERS

The combination of fruit with flowers has intrigued artists for centuries. Paintings of these together have been a source of inspiration to all who study the paintings of the early Dutch and Flemish masters. There is some intrinsic quality in the bloom on fruit which is completely complementary to the softer texture of flowers, and nowhere is this seen more clearly than against the dark, mysterious background common to most of these early paintings. In most of them there is a richness rendered either by the fruit itself (gleaming drops, for instance, from a peeled lemon which would seldom be practicable in a live arrangement!) or by some object not necessarily relative to the subject-matter.

I feel, therefore, that this form of decoration calls for a special type of background and is not a combination for a casual flower arrangement.

The cone of fruit and flowers illustrated here was an example of several which decorated a buffet in the historic Merchant Taylor's Hall which is described in the last chapter of this book. The occasion and the setting were an opportunity for decorations of this type and the one photographed here is in similar surroundings.

The flowers, fruit and berries were wired into a cone of damp moss as described in Chapter 8 and, despite the fact that this was pure floristry, the cone kept its elegance and bloom for several days until finally the roses faded. Although these 'Ophelia' roses were the only ordinary flowers used, the two varieties of echeverias gave an effect of flowers. I have found that the wax-like texture and marbled shadings of many species of succulent plants bring harmony between the bloom on fruit and the matt petals of flowers. The large green echeveria in the centre is *E. glauca*, and the six small, paler variety, which are embedded among the roses, are *E. derenbergii*. Some species of sedum have the same formation, and *S. weinbergii* is one of the loveliest I have seen as it has leaves which could have been carved from pale pink marble. Indeed, for those who find fascination in tones of subtle grey, rose-grey and blue-green, and in textures that are wax-like and yet of luminous delicacy, I would advocate a collection of these lovely things for a frost-free greenhouse.

NEAT DESIGNS FOR CHRISTMAS

The decorations illustrated here require a measure of floristry in their making and full details with diagrams are given in Chapter 10. They show, I think, how effective the traditional holly and gaudy baubles associated with the Christmas festival can be when they are confined to neat and attractive designs.

Variegated holly was used for the wreath and little tree in this photograph as it has a lighter and more gay effect than the usual green variety. It is, however, not so easy to find, but green holly can be lightened by touching the edges of the leaves with paint or by brushing part of them with gum or varnish and then sprinkling over with silver glitter.

It is sometimes necessary to add extra berries to holly decorations and I feel that artificial ones are permissible on these occasions. Alternatively, sprays of glittering beads made into the form of flowers can augment the decoration as shown on the wreath. All that is required for these are strings of brilliant-coloured Christmas beads, together with a few stub wires or thick fuse wire. The beads are threaded on to the required lengths of wire, which are then bent into oblong shapes and the two ends twisted together to form a stem. Five or six are then grouped round a larger bauble (bundles of these can be bought already conveniently mounted on wire stems) and the whole lot wired firmly together to form the 'flower'.

Similar (and cheaper) 'flowers' can be made by forming the loops from wire which has first been gummed and then dipped into glitter and grouping them round a silvered seed-head or tiny fir-cone. Indeed, the permutations are endless for those with inventive minds.

Candles are an essential part of Christmas table decorations, and if they are placed among beads and baubles there is not the same fire risk as when they are in the midst of painted dried material. Here the cones have been made of plasticine into which the candles were firmly inserted. They can, of course, be renewed if necessary, as the beads are arranged in descending circles from around the candlehole.

I was asked to decorate a marquee which enclosed a circular sunk garden, edged by yew hedges, with beds of pink roses and four large completely round box trees. Immediately an idea for its decoration sprang to mind; the garden would be acccentuated by placing four small box balls on top of the existing ones in the manner of topiary trees, and all of them would be closely studded with pink roses similar to those growing in the garden. No other decoration was necessary. On the night of the dance spotlights shone down on the spectacular round rose trees which, in their exaggeration of nature, magnified the illusion of an enchanted garden, and, indeed, many guests were uncertain as to whether everything was real or was part of a planned and made-up décor.

Marquees vary very considerably and range from plain canvas tents to elaborate built-out rooms complete with doors and windows and ball-room fittings, devised by the great tent manufacturers. More usually, however, we are called upon to decorate the type of marquee which is interlined with, and has a draped ceiling of a pretty striped material. Any central poles should be covered with the same material, as they then require no decoration as camouflage. Generally speaking, the walls of these marquees are only about six feet high, so that if any pedestal arrangements are required they must be kept low. On occasions a really large all-round arrangement in the centre of a marquee is very effective as there is height here to take a pedestal group. A vase and stand which resembles lead or stone is attractive for such a decoration, as it can look as if it was a garden fixture around which the marquee had been built. It is always advisable to use weighted pedestals in marquees as the floor is often uneven and there is more risk than usual of decorations being knocked over.

When opportunity offers, however, I think less stereotyped arrangements are preferable. Indeed, the decoration of a marquee can be a challenge to our ingenuity as, for such a transitory occasion, gay and unusual adornments can be contrived from materials that are neither long-lasting nor expensive, and use can be made of swags and garlands, baskets of flowers and rose-ball trees that could in fact be real. As none of these require more florist's skill than that which is described at the end of Chapter 2, I offer the following basic details which can be elaborated according to the type of decoration required.

Swags and garlands

These can be made entirely from greenery, entirely of flowers or a combination of both, and are effective in a number of ways. Swags, which are
wider and heavier than garlands, can be used as pelmets with side drops
over doors or windows, as curved loops between light fixtures, or as a
decoration for the front of a raised platform. The easiest method of making
them is to bind the material on to long strips of folded newspaper as
described for holly and evergreen wreaths in Chapter 9. If a definite shape
is required, such as a curved pelmet over a door or window, then it is advisable to cut out the design in small-mesh wire-netting on to which damp
moss is firmly bound with green string. The greenery or flower-heads are
then pegged on to this with two-inch wires bent to form a hairpin, or,
alternatively, ordinary straight thick hairpins could be used. Garlands can
be made by binding the flowers on to very narrow rolls of newspaper, but
the more usual method is to bind the material directly on to the required
lengths of rope or thick string. Care must be taken, however, to keep these
flat while being made up, as otherwise they can become twisted. Garlands
are effective when spiralled round posts or pillars, hung in loops right round
a marquee or used as a decoration for the front of a buffet.

Baskets

Baskets of garden flowers make one of the prettiest and most suitable
decorations for a marquee. They can be hung at intervals round the walls,
suspended from the cross-beams on ribbon-covered cord. There are hazards,
however, as a basket which is suspended against what can often be a wind-
swept canvas wall is not the easiest form of container in which to arrange
flowers. A flat back is really essential, and as there are not so many to be
found that are shaped in this way a cheap bicycle basket can be quite a
satisfactory substitute. Baskets with no linings can be covered inside with
polythene, which holds damp Florapak quite successfully for short periods,
and a layer of wire-netting should be firmly tied over the top. Whatever the
shape, I think a basket needs an abundance of flowers. A formal design is
out of place for this type of arrangement and the flowers should spill
lavishly in all directions, the more simple and garden-like the better.

Rose ball trees

As I have said, these little trees have proved immensely successful as decorations in marquees. They are gay and pretty, stand firm on the ground, occupy little space and, at first glance, could be real trees brought in from the garden for the occasion. The first steps, however, are not easy and if the man of the house is a handyman his help could well be enlisted. The following are required for each tree:

1. A small wooden tub about nine inches high by eleven inches wide, preferably painted white with black bands, or a large flowerpot similarly painted.
2. A straight sapling about 3½ feet long by one inch diameter.
3. Four small, firm sticks cut to fit the width of the tub a third from the top.
4. Enough moss to make a football-sized ball.
5. Wire-netting and green string.
6. Cement or Polyfilla and wet sand.

The first and most important point is to get the sapling firmly wedged into the tub, which should be sufficiently weighted to prevent the finished tree from over-balancing it. Place the sapling in the exact centre of the tub and wedge it there with the four small sticks as shown in Figure 31. The tub should now be filled with cement for a depth of three to four inches in order to hold the sapling in place and to supply the necessary weight. Cement, however, is not a practicable commodity for everyone so Polyfilla can be used (rather more expensively) instead, but the tub will subsequently need the additional weight of wet sand. The top is made by working a piece of pliable wire-netting into the shape of a ball, about the size of a small football, with the bottom left open. A small square of wood should be affixed to the top end (to prevent the point of the sapling working through) and the wire ball is then partially filled with moss and placed over the sapling as shown in Figure 32. Additional moss is pressed into the ball until it is completely full and firm to the touch, when the open end should be closed by pressing the ends of the wire-netting firmly together. Finally the moss is thoroughly sprayed so that it is damp right through, and the ball is now ready for decoration. About six to eight dozen roses will be required to cover such a ball completely, but these can be of the cheapest variety as

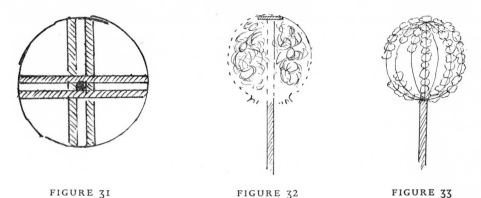

FIGURE 31   FIGURE 32   FIGURE 33

virtually only the heads are used. Alternatively, the ball can be covered
entirely in greenery and merely studded with roses, when half the above
quantity will be required, but in either case it is necessary to put leaves
on first. Sprays of rose leaves are charming, but unfortunately they go limp
very quickly so that sprays of any small evergreen leaves are preferable.
These are pegged into place with hairpin-bent wires. The roses are mounted
through the calyx described in Chapter 2, Figure 20, and are then inserted
into the moss. Unlike cones, these rose balls should not appear too symmetrical and are prettier if the roses are mounted on slightly differing
lengths of stem to give an in-and-out effect. Equally, it would appear
unnatural if they were inserted in circles from the top, so it is better to get
the required shape by quartering the ball like an orange as in Figure 33 and
then to fill in the gaps where necessary. Although roses are the perfect
flowers for these tub trees, any rounded flowers—such as carnations, pompon dahlias, small zinnias or African marigolds—are also quite effective,
but, of course, the tree is then only a ball of flowers and not, as it can appear
with roses, a seemingly natural tree. In a pure white marquee these trees
can be eye-catching if they are entirely green with long swags and wall-
drops made of the same greenery.

When completed, the rose balls should be sprayed and covered with
damp tissue paper until required. And when the party is over, and the
flowers and leaves removed, the mossed balls should be dampened and
enclosed completely in polythene bags ready for use on another occasion.
In fact, if the moss is dampened periodically these trees will remain intact

indefinitely and can be used in a variety of ways with different material. For instance, if the stem is covered with scarlet ribbon and the moss balls with gold painted leaves or natural variegated holly, the tree becomes an attractive Christmas decoration to stand by the newel post of a pretty staircase.

Wedding receptions

For a wedding reception rather more formal decorations are required than some of those described in the preceding pages, although swags and garlands are always suitable decorations for a marquee. It is usual to have either one or two arrangements of flowers immediately behind the bride and groom but, if the reception is in a marquee, a central arrangement is generally more effective.

The wedding cake can be made quite a feature, especially if placed on a table by itself. The picture between pages 104 and 105 shows a frilled organza cloth with three small posies of flowers trimming the ruffled swag. For this occasion rings of flowers were hung on to a small beribboned stick in the manner of an *epergne* (which would make a charming supper-table decoration), but similar rings could be placed round the tiers of a wedding cake with a rounded bouquet of similar flowers for the top tier.

Flowers for parties take time, but such expenditure is worth while as lovely and memorable decorations add considerably to the success of the occasion. Indeed, whether the party is to be gay or formal, simple or elaborate, I think the underlying principle remains the same, namely that it is, in effect, an occasion for celebration and therefore any means employed to heighten the enjoyment of those concerned is fully justifiable.

9. Church Decorations

Churches are places of solemnity whatever their size. Decorations of a formal type generally seem most suitable and it is better to have a few large arrangements rather than too many small ones. Line is of particular importance, and where the design of an arrangement can follow the curve of an arch, or emphasize the grace of a pillar, it can become an inherent part of the church itself instead of a superimposed decoration.

The weekly decorations are normally the prerogative of special members of the congregation, but it is rare for these people, who have the real affection for their church at heart, to have the time to study flower arrangement in all its aspects. On certain ceremonial occasions, when rather special decorations are necessary, they may feel uncertain how to go about the matter. For those, and for the many others who have occasion to decorate a church for a particular ceremony, I will try to answer the questions I have been asked so often and mention the problems that have beset me myself.

To decorate a church for a great occasion two things should be borne in mind: first, that a really big architecturally beautiful church generally requires fewer arrangements than a small one, and that these should be formal in line and of a size and height to conform to the background; secondly, that an effect of simplicity is desirable in small churches, particularly country ones, and that these can be more gaily bedecked with flowers and advantage taken of wide window-sills, candle-sconces among the pews, or lovely old pew ends, all of which can be adorned with flowers.

When contemplating a decoration for a wedding it is essential to meet the persons concerned at the church beforehand, when the colour scheme and type of arrangement can be discussed. It is desirable that the church flowers should tone with those carried either by the bride, or her brides-maids, and it is preferable that the style in both decorating and floristry should be the same throughout. It is advisable to have the Rector or Vicar or Priest at this meeting, as many churches have their own special customs and one should not work in opposition to them. At this meeting it is a good thing to arrange when it would be most convenient to do the decorations and when the clearing should be done. Normally the big London churches are cleared immediately after the service, but in the country flowers are frequently left over the week-end. In both cases it is usual to leave the altar flowers for the church, which is the reason why the authorities concerned prefer their own vases, and these rarely consist nowadays of the awkward brass bottle-necked variety which was the custom only a few years ago. Equally they may fear unsuitability in the choice of vases on the part of the decorator, and most decorators have to suffer for the mistakes of those who have gone before them. The small urn illustrated between pages 136 and 137 is an example of the type of vase acceptable in most churches, and here it has been filled with garden lilac, stripped of heavy leaves, and *Lilium longiflorum*. It is worth remembering that altar vases are generally seen from a lower level, so it is advisable to let some of the central material droop well forward, almost to the level of the altar, otherwise the 'faces' of the flowers will not be seen.

Weddings in great churches

Symmetry is important where there is grandeur and space. If funds permit, I like to see pairs of groups leading the way to the altar in the manner of an avenue of flowers. It is usual for two groups to stand on either side of the chancel steps, although these can often bar the way to the pulpit and necessitate the moving of the lectern. Both these requiremants are generally permissible provided the vases are moved before the next service. Sufficient space must be left here for four people to stand comfortably between the groups. Slightly closer together two more groups can stand at some point between the chancel steps and the altar, the apex of the avenue converging on the altar flowers.

As it is important that the flowers should be seen after the arrival of the guests the groups should start at shoulder-level at least, and be as high as the occasion demands. Pedestals can be anything from three feet upwards and are best in a neutral tone, such as pale grey, which will merge into the background of a church. The most suitable vases are wide-lipped and of classical design. A matt-surfaced pottery is preferable for most occasions, although such beautiful mediums as marble, stone and alabaster can be used in those places where the vases are a permanent feature of the church. Metal linings, with handles, can be made for these, in order to avoid any damage which might occur through moving the vases themselves. Sometimes the font is in a strategic place, just by the entrance, and then it is worth obtaining the permission of the authorities to put a group on it. The lid of the font is often beautifully carved and embellished, but this can generally be turned upside down to form a level base. Alternatively, a tray or wooden board can be fitted over the top.

When considering the position of groups in a church it is, of course, desirable that some background be found when possible, and if a pillar is conveniently placed, or there is a rood- or chancel-screen, then the flowers show to better advantage, and require less material, than groups in an open position. On the whole, however, groups in big churches have to be in the open to attain the necessary symmetry and, if well arranged, can be unbelievably lovely when light shines on them. It should, however, be remembered that such groups require more flowers than those with a background behind them. It is desirable that groups in churches should be, as nearly as possible, in the form of identical pairs. It is best, therefore, to put the outline in both vases before proceeding further.

Because of the height required for church groups it is generally necessary to use florist's tubes for some flowers, but these should be used most sparingly as they naturally tend to artificiality. I rarely use more than two, even in the largest group, and these should be inserted vertically, and extremely firmly, in front of the spinal stem. It is essential, to my mind, that only tall-growing flowers should be used in tubes for the highest point, as so often small flowers, which could not possibly reach such heights of growth, are carried to the top of the arrangement by tube and immediately the natural look is gone and the group becomes unreal. Artifices must be used on some occasions, but in decorating it is best to do without them except in real necessity. The wiring of flowers is intended for floristry, a highly skilled and technical art, and should not be used here except for such flowers as zinnias, which have a habit of strangling themselves, or the occasional very recalcitrant tulip.

As with all arrangements, and particularly large ones, great care should be taken to ensure that the stems forming the outline are well balanced and firmly placed in the vase. On no account should any of them be unsteady, as they form the framework on which the group is built. I have found that it is advisable to use a heavier-gauge wire-netting for really big arrangements, as it remains firm even under the weight of heavy branches. For extra safety I also tie the wire-netting to the vase, either across the top and round under the rim or attached to the handles should it possess them. The string is hidden later by the flowers.

The number of flowers required for a large arrangement often presents a problem to people who are not in the habit of doing such arrangements regularly. As a guide the following list is typical of what would be needed for a June wedding arrangement (normally one of a pair) in an average-sized church.

Five long stems of foliage such as stripped lime, Whitebeam or young beech.
Seven stems of delphinium for the 'spine' and sides lines.
Twelve long stems of double stock for filling in the outline.
Three stems of Candidum lilies, a dozen peonies and three artichoke or arum leaves for the centre.
The addition of a few trailing stems of flowering shrubs, such as philadelphus or escallonia, add considerable grace to any arrangement on a stand.

Weddings in small churches

It is, I think, even more important to view a small church before deciding on a scheme of decoration, than it is a big one. Each is entirely different and very often may possess some outstanding feature which is worth emphasizing. If the proportions and symmetry of a great church are there, then I think it is right to decorate it in the same formal manner. On the other hand, in country churches in particular, there is generally so much more light that flowers seem necessary in places other than the chancel. Window-

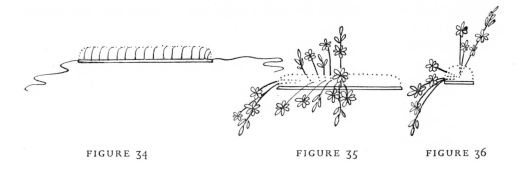

FIGURE 34   FIGURE 35   FIGURE 36

sills can be decorated and, if the sill is sloping and unsuitable for a vase, mossed pads of flowers can generally be attached to some part of the sill from which flowers can then cascade in any shape desired. (Figures 34–36 illustrate this.) Admittedly this form of decoration necessitates some experience of floristry, but even a rudimentary knowledge of the first steps given in Chapter 2 would be sufficient for the wiring and mounting of flowers for such a purpose.

Sometimes posies tied to pew ends seem desirable. They can be unbelievably pretty for a summer wedding and are not difficult to make. Rounded, loose bunches of flowers can be attached to the pew ends and tied off with suitable ribbon. Mossed pads of flowers are, however, infinitely preferable. For these, a few handfuls of moss are firmly bound together with green string, one side being kept flat. Double-strength lengths of string are left free for tying in place round the pews. The flat side should be covered with polythene or cellophane to prevent marks being left on surfaces. Suitable flowers and foliages are then mounted on wire legs and inserted into the moss in an oblong shape. (See Figures 37–39.) When tied to the pew ends the strings can be covered by ribbon to tone with the flowers, or can be hidden beneath a ledge of moulding or carving.

Some really old country churches have beautiful candle-sconces rising at intervals between the pews. On these occasions I generally advise that they should be decorated with little crowns of flowers, as these are carried high above the heads of the guests and look almost as if they were suspended in the air. Small flowers and leaves are required for these and, as

123

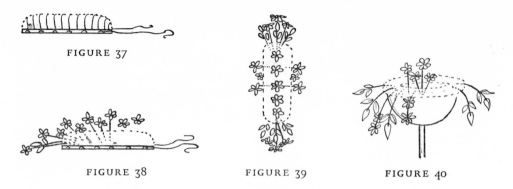

FIGURE 37

FIGURE 38

FIGURE 39

FIGURE 40

they are seen from below, it is important that the material should be bent well down over the outer edge in order to hide the moss. (See Figure 40.) While making these rings it is easiest to place them on top of a jam-jar so that the correct droop can be ascertained. If they are packed on suitably-sized mounds of tissue paper, they will come to no harm before being dropped into place over the top of the candles. Provided the flowers are of reasonably lasting varieties, any of these mossed arrangements can be made the day before they are required. They should be left in a cool place, preferably on a stone floor, and after a good spraying should be covered with damp tissue paper.

Here are some suggested requirements for each of the foregoing arrangements:

A window-sill pad in mixed white flowers for a spring wedding

A length of wood or small-mesh wire-netting about 12 in. × 2 in., on one side of which moss is firmly bound and double string it attached to the ends for tying in place.

Three stems of camellia or small evergreen foliage.

Seven firm stems of common ivy.

Three small bergenia leaves.

One bunch of dwarf gladioli 'The Bride'.

Three stems of pompon chrysanthemum spray or bunch of early stock.

One dozen carnations.

One bunch of short double tulips 'Snow Queen'.

One bunch of strong freesias, like 'White Swan', or a few cynthella hyacinths.

First put in the shape with the camellia and ivy, allowing the latter to flow well down from the central front. Follow the outline with the gladioli in graduated lengths, and fill in with the spray or stock and finally the carnations, using some of the latter for the central cascade. The bergenia leaves and tulips should make a rounded centre out of which come the spray of freesias or cynthella hyacinths.

A pew-pad in mixed pink flowers for a summer wedding

A round mossed pad, flat at the back, about 5 in. in diameter.
Six stems of pale grey foliage such as *Senecio laxifolius* or 'Glacier' variegated ivy.
Three small glaucous hosta leaves.
Six stems of dwarf gladioli 'Peachblossom'
One bunch of short pink stock.
One dozen 'Carol' roses.
Six tiny pink arums or pips of Regale lilies.

A pew-pad must be much firmer in shape than one for a window-sill and should not extend sideways beyond the width of the pew. It can, however, drip downwards as far as proportion and flowers permit. These are illustrated in the picture between pages 136 and 137, which shows a small country church bedecked with flowers for a summer wedding.

Rings for candle-sconces

The mossed rings should be big enough to slip easily over the candle after the flowers have been inserted.
For single sconces each ring would require approximately :
Six pieces of either small-leaved ivy, thyme or sedum, variegated geranium or maidenhair, anything in fact that can be made to droop gracefully from the outer edge of the ring.
About six spiky flowers to give height, such as Kaffir lilies, miniature daffodils, freesias, clusters of lily of the valley, pink salvias, heathers or side-shoots of delphinium or larkspur.
Seed-heads or berries can be used in the autumn or winter.

About a dozen small rounded flowers, preferably on budded stems, for filling in. These could be Christmas or Lenten roses, anemones, ranunculus, miniature roses, pinks, French marigolds, 'Tom thumb' zinnias, or pompon dahlias and chrysanthemums.

Any work that requires a measure of floristry requires time and patience, but a change from stereotyped arrangements can be very welcome. Although these are but a few suggestions, they are an indication of the scope that exists for a varied but suitable approach to the decoration of different types of churches.

Christenings

In general only the font is decorated for a christening. Some churches possess specially made tins which fit in a semi-circle either round the top of the font or at a slightly lower level. When this is the case decoration is simple, and small flowers, with neat leaves and foliage, can be arranged directly into the tins with sufficient trailing foliage to hide the outside. If these are not available, then I think a mossed frame made to fit three-quarters of the way round the font is preferable to anything else. Suitable flowers and foliages are mounted on wire legs and inserted into the moss before the decoration is taken to the church. The whole frame can then be easily removed when the christening is over. In spring-time nothing is more charming for such an occasion than tiny bunches of spring flowers inserted in groups, making, as it were, a miniature garden. An arrangement at the base of the font is not so suitable, as it cannot always be seen by all those present.

Christmas

At Christmas-time it is not unusual for those in charge of the decorations to find themselves in possession of an over-abundance of holly and evergreens, and probably of helpers too. The final decorations can look disappointingly untidy, so I offer the following suggestions for those who have both ample material and sufficient assistance available. As at all times a note of dignity and formality is desirable in church decorations, it is perhaps preferable to see holly and evergreens formed into wreaths and garlands rather than bunched into vases or festooned over any available projections. Wreaths and garlands are neither messy nor difficult to make with the help of old newspapers and green garden twine. This is the method by which they are made:

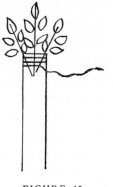

Lay three large sheets of opened newspaper on top of each other and fold them lengthwise to form a three-inch-wide roll. Cut pieces of holly or evergreen into three-inch pieces, removing damaged leaves and any dead wood. Starting at the end farthest from you, attach the string firmly and bind the pieces on to one side in neat rows so that they completely cover the paper. (See Figure 41.) The string should be given a sharp tug at

FIGURE 41

the end of each row to ensure firmness. Allow a few inches at the end to overlap with the beginning of the roll and form into a circle, firmly binding the ends together.

Garlands can be most effective if they are spiralled round pillars or hung in loops beneath windows. They can be made in the same way as the wreaths, but with only two layers of paper folded into a roll about two inches wide. These can be joined together to reach any length desired, and are more easy to handle than garlands made of rope as they do not twist and lose their shape.

If holly berries are scarce, additional decoration can be added by bunches of red Silsheen ribbon or a few artificial berries can be added discreetly. This, however, is rarely necessary, as the shape of the wreaths and garlands is a decoration in itself and combines equally well with Christmas trees or arrangements of fresh flowers or evergreens.

Some suitable types of flowers and foliages

Although it would be quite impossible to give a comprehensive list of suitable flowers for church decoration at all seasons, I would like to suggest some types of flowers and foliages which have proved particularly useful to me. Nor is it necessary here to restrict one's choice to what is available in the garden as for such arrangements one can generally choose from what the shops and greenhouses have to offer too.

For backing there is nothing, in my opinion, to surpass spring blossom, lightly trimmed of its leaves. It is ethereal in effect, glorious in the manner of its growth, and branches can be gently pruned to achieve every shape imaginable. For white groups there is the common cherry, both single and double, followed by many varieties of white prunus and malus (crab). Among the viburnums the 'Snow-Ball' tree, or guelder rose, is invaluable both in its early green stage and when the snow-balls develop to pure white. For church groups, philadelphus (Mock Orange) is more decorative to my mind than any other form of blossom. Long wands of this lovely shrub, trimmed of heavy leaves, make the perfect background for spring and early summer flowers. Adaptable to any design, the sweetly-scented flower-laden branches are perfection in themselves and should not be obscured by the flowers that complete the group. *P. × lemoinei* v. 'Virginal', which has large double flowers, was used to outline the pedestal groups shown in the illustration between pages 136 and 137. For yellow groups there is early *Hamamelis mollis* (witch-hazel), *Cornus mas* (cornelian cherry), forsythia in variety and *Kerria japonica*, and for the pink groups all tones of pink almond, plum and cherry, from the early *Prunus cerasifera* 'Nigra' to the many varieties of Japanese cherry, among which I find the drooping stems of 'Kiku Shidare' particularly useful. There is now a lovely true pink lilac which is invaluable among pink or pastel groups.

It has been my privilege to decorate on several occasions a beautiful and ancient church where the great east window in the chancel has framed a pink cherry tree in full bloom. Despite its antiquity this church is full of light, and groups of similar blossom were arranged in pairs from the chancel steps to the altar, making an avenue of flowers in line with the lovely tree beyond, to which all eyes were lifted.

When blossom is available the centres of such groups should be light, and nothing is more in keeping than *Lilium longiflorum*, the budded stems of which can be the topmost point and the open flowers the focal centre. Arums, together with their leaves, are invaluable at this time of year when the spring flowers are still too small for really big groups. A stem or two of Hippeastrum (amaryllis) can also be a main feature for a big group, and they range in colour from white, through pinks and flames, to crimson. As spring advances, rhododendrons become available in all their species and when stripped of redundant leaves are very suitable for inclusion in such arrangements. Later still come the giant peony-flowered tulips of which, like their namesake, nothing has more value in decoration. White 'Mount Tacoma', pink 'Eros' and yellow 'Gold Medal' are specially desirable, as they have the necessary size and length of stem. These immense tulips are rarely seen in shop-windows, which is a pity, as they are easy to grow and long-lasting when cut. Their inclusion in any garden is well worth while.

The old-fashioned Crown Imperials (*Fritillaria imperialis*) are not used now in decoration as much as they deserve to be. Ranging in colour from pale yellow to bronze, their stately drooping heads are massive enough for inclusion in the largest arrangement.

When summer comes we have such a host of flowers to choose from that sometimes it is difficult to keep one's head and avoid too miscellaneous an arrangement. Against the majesty of great churches too much variation is undesirable. Indeed, nothing can be more beautiful (if funds permit) than immense regal groups of lilies, alone with their leaves or some suitable foliage. Peonies are perhaps the most useful of all early summer flowers for decorative purposes. The double ones are best suited to church groups and, while they are available, the problem of the open-faced flowers does not arise.

The long-stemmed spray chrysanthemums, which are now available throughout the year, are of untold value in all big arrangements. I use them most gratefully through autumn to spring, but amongst the abundance of summer flowers they seem a little out of place. This is doubtless a perverse and personal prejudice, as I welcome roses at all times, but during the brief months of plenty I like to use flowers that are essentially typical of their season: such as white delphiniums, gladioli, foxgloves and the stately eremurus, sweet-scented stocks, Candidum lilies and pink-tinged Regale lilies, and whenever possible, multitudes of huge, blossoming garden roses. One of the most beautiful flowers for really big church arrangements is the Auratum lily. Available through most of the summer and autumn months, it lends nobility and grace to any group. I have used it alone with stripped lime and huge leaves, and it is particularly lovely in cream arrangements verging to pale yellow and gold.

Sometimes in the summer suitable foliage is not so easy to find as at other times, despite the abundance all around us. Equally, neither is it so necessary as so many more flowers are available. The introduction of greens and greys is, nevertheless, generally necessary and, even if foliage is not required for backing, we may need something to trail, or lend a lovely line beyond the length of the flowers. Young beech and silvery grey Whitebeam (both of which can be found on a country walk), lime branches stripped of leaves to show the slender flower pods, pale variegated privet or variegated ivy are all suitable in early summer, and shrubs such as the trailing feathery *Stephanandra tanakae*, covered in minute creamy yellow flowers, pink or white escallonia or pink kalmia lend distinction to any group.

Leaves are a valuable addition at all times. Those of the arum are well known, and of equal value—particularly in white and pale pink groups—are the grey artichoke, 'Cardoon' and onopordon leaves which are serrated at the edges and statuesque in shape.

As summer moves into autumn we have dahlias in all their clear colours, and there are many white varieties which are superb for church decoration. Hydrangeas and white agapanthus also provide large rounded heads which are so useful for the centres of big groups. White crinums and, later, white 'Belladonna' lilies have a clear wax-like beauty most suitable for churches.

Because of their long-lasting qualities and great range of colour, I think we are apt to rely too much on chrysanthemums in autumn. Until the frosts wreak their final havoc, let us use the last of the clear-toned summer flowers and, when funds permit, the lilies like *L. longiflorum* or *L. rubrum*, which are almost perennially with us and which can add such elegance to formal arrangements. Rayonnante chrysanthemums, with their delicate spidery petals and subtle colours, are much lighter in formation than others of their species, and are well worth the extra cost involved. Later in the autumn the lovely marguerite-like singles begin to appear, of which the soft pink 'Vedova' and the apricot-coloured 'Olnura' are excellent varieties.

Branches of berries give both lightness and richness to autumn groups and, like hips and haws and the many wild viburnums, can be gathered from the hedgerows as well as from the vast group of berried garden shrubs. Snowberries and white pernettyas are particularly good for white decorations and there is a great choice among the berberises and cotoneasters to tone with the richer-coloured schemes.

Shining camellia foliage is beautiful for backing where the background is light, but it is wasteful to use it when the church is dark. This also applies to myrtle. In mid-winter, when the backing for white groups presents a real problem, I have attached small skeleton magnolia leaves to bare beech branches and made with them (admittedly artificially) the most ethereal and graceful of backgrounds. Dried honesty can be used in conjunction with these, as its silver petals have the same transparent quality and are a foil to the dull transparency of the magnolia leaves. Grevillia foliage is useful too, with small pointed leaves which are green on one side and silver on the other, and the many varieties of grey eucalyptus foliage fit in with any scheme.

During the months before Christmas it is often hard to find suitable flowers as points to our groups, and then the sword-like leaves of New Zealand Flax (*Phormium tenax*) are invaluable. They are of a shining pale green outlined in cream and show up against any background.

The long varieties of nerines are large enough for many church groups and have value in that they add lightness to winter arrangements. Poinsettias are one of my favourite winter flowers, and they are truly spectacular in big groups. The pale pink and green-white varieties are even more lovely than the well-known scarlet, but they need careful treatment if they are to last well, and require a deep drink in hot water before being arranged.

Colour

My personal preference is for pale flowers in a church. They are light-giving and show up well even though the day may be dark. Mixed white flowers have a pearl-like quality and are, I think,, unsurpassed for a wedding service. Pale pinks, yellows and all pastel colours are equally suitable, but blues are best used in conjunction with other shades as they are apt to lose their colour in poor or artificial light. The paler tones of apricot and flame, buffs and tawny yellows are especially beautiful in the autumn, but really dark reds or bronzes are generally best avoided as they can look black and leave, as it were, a gap in the arrangement.

To sum up, proportion is all-important in big churches. Line should be clearly defined and, where possible, integrated with the architectural features. Material should be large. Small flowers are lost in arrangements of this size and particular emphasis, with large-headed flowers and big leaves, should be concentrated on the centre of such groups. In small churches some deviation from accepted ideas is often desirable. Decorations can be pretty rather than imposing and, in country churches particularly, it is best to maintain an effect of simplicity.

But whether in grandeur or simplicity, I think that church decorations should adhere to some formality. It is better to have too few arrangements properly in accord with their surroundings than too many placed irrelevantly in every available space. For great occasions decorations should be high enough to be seen when the church is full and, where possible, placed where they can become inherently part of the church itself.

In conclusion, I would like to repeat a word of warning. Perfection in tidying up is important everywhere, but nowhere is it more so than in a church; a single green leaf carelessly disregarded can stain a stone or marble floor for weeks to come, and water spilt on an altar cloth can do irreparable harm.

IO. Christmas Decorations

Christmas decorations have moved a long way in recent years from the traditional green of holly and mistletoe and the candle-lit tree. Almost as autumn ends the shops begin to dazzle us with the glitter of tinsel and jewel-like baubles and to startle us with the novelty of their schemes. Indeed, it seems that they vie with each other to produce something different and, in so doing, are in danger at times of losing a part of the original concept of Christmas. It would appear that anything is permissible at this time and that fantasy has free rein, but I think the question of suitability is just as important in regard to Christmas decorations as it is with flower decorations. Many friendly, comfortable houses, where children abound, seem to require the traditional present-laden tree and the berried abundance of holly and mistletoe. Others are so modern that only stark branches and baubles seem in place. But for most of us something in between is necessary. Personally, I like lightness and if we can reproduce the ethereal effect of frost on trees and hedgerows, and hold it in our houses for a while, then surely we have caught something of the traditional idea of Christmas.

Frosted arrangements

The vogue for whitening and glittering trees, twigs, leaves and seed-heads has opened up endless possibilities for us all. Really lovely effects can be achieved at little cost if we use our ingenuity and are nimble-fingered. It is, of course, possible to buy material that has already been painted, but there is not the same satisfaction in bought decorations as there is in those you have done yourself. Nor is it possible to find a variety in the shops comparable to that which is available to any of us who possess a garden or who are selective on a country walk.

We must all have marvelled at some time or other at the cobweb tracery of frost on trees, which obliterates the solid stems and branches with a mask of semi-transparency and reduces all to a ghost world. It is possible to simulate this effect by whitening and glittering dried leaves and foliages just enough to reproduce the appearance of frost. A selection of different types should be chosen for a design in just the same manner as for an arrangement of mixed flowers. Strong stems are necessary for the outline, among which apple tree, larch or lichen-covered branches are excellent. Ferns of any sort, such as osmunda, the common fern and bracken, which have been previously dried and pressed between newspapers, are perfect for filling in the background. Pointed yucca leaves (but avoid their sharp edges) and the more solid cycas leaves are good for background, too. The following types of material are also useful for filling in: dried corn, barley, teazles, small bulrushes, artichoke and onion heads, poppy and lily seed-pods, dried hydrangeas, big and little fir cones and, in fact, anything from the garden or countryside that dries well and is substantial enough to take paint and glitter.

Both solid and transparent material is generally required for the centre of the arrangements. The evergreen leaves of *Magnolia grandiflora*, rhododendron and laurel keep their shape when painted and last a long time without shrivelling. And for the true transparency reminiscent of frost there is nothing to equal skeleton magnolia leaves, however commercialized they may have become. They can be left in their natural colour, with just the tips glittered, or delicately gilded or silvered. When they are mounted on wires for use as leaves, or made into chalice-like flowers with centres of tiny fir-cones or seed-pods, they play a major part in decorations of this type. Preserved *adiantum* (maidenhair) has also the necessary ethereal quality for this type of work and can be treated in the same manner as the magnolia leaves.

Essential equipment

Some knowledge of floristry is helpful in the making of most Christmas decorations. Although it can take years to become really proficient in this delicate art with real flowers, considerable skill can be achieved quite quickly with the material suitable for these decorations, and the suggestions given in Chapter 2 may prove helpful. Florists' tools are not always readily available to everyone but, if possible, it is worth procuring some stub scissors (which cut wires as well as flowers), some stub wires, the most useful being 20 in. or 22 in. by 12 in., and a reel of medium silver wire. White or natural coloured gutter is useful for covering the stems, but it is possible to improvise with strips of crêpe paper and cards of fuse wire can substitute for silver wire. It is advisable to buy good glitter as it does not tarnish, and many decorations can be put away in tissue paper to be used another year.

Depending on the scheme envisaged, some of the following will be required:

A tin of flat white paint or under-coating.
Gold and silver paint or lacquer.
Gold and silver glitter.
A bottle of turpentine.
A tin of clear varnish and, for very delicate work, a bottle of clear nail varnish.
A tube of clear Bostik glue.
Sand, or small stones, to weight the vases, which can otherwise easily upset as they do not contain water.
Some cheap paint brushes and, if possible, a small paint spray.
And finally, and perhaps most desirable of all, an attic or cellar where the inevitable mess need not be cleared away and painted material can be left to dry.

Although everything can be either sprayed with a paint spray or painted by brush, I think it is best, if a choice is possible, to spray such things as trees, branches, hydrangeas and seed-heads and to paint delicate material like ferns and leaves. The material is best painted on a flat surface, reverse side first, and then held over a clean piece of paper to be glittered. This avoids waste, as the surplus glitter can be collected for use again. Any table will do to work on and, if it is well protected with newspaper, it will come to no harm. It is helpful to have shelves, trays or a spare table at hand on which to lay the newly-painted material to dry. Upright stemmed material can be dried in tall jars or cans filled with sand or loose wire-netting.

Christmas trees

The white Christmas tree, apparently, has come to stay and looks better in many houses than the traditional green one. It can be quite small and yet, when decorated in keeping with its surroundings, is symbolic of Christmas. A well-shaped, rather fully-branched tree should be chosen for whitening. This can be done with distemper or flat white paint. A spray is desirable but an old Flit gun will serve quite well. The tree should be firmly planted in a pot filled with sand or stones, and wedged, if necessary, with pieces of wood. Frosting or glitter can be sprinkled over the tree while the paint is still wet and this adds considerably to the effect. White trees can, of course, be decorated according to any taste, but they look best, in my opinion, if the colours chosen pick up some salient feature in the room. Equally, white always looks wonderful if decorated only with gold and silver, or, alternatively, very pale opal colours give a glistening impression of frost which is often far more effective than the more usual red and white colour scheme so much in demand at Christmas.

Rather more ambitious, and certainly much more expensive, are trees made from plastic ferns. On the other hand, they will last indefinitely and thereby repay the initial cost and trouble. Plastic ferns can be bought from many flower shops prior to Christmas and the pure white ones are best for this purpose. These are attached by wire covered in white crêpe paper (as shown in Figures 42–44) to a firm stem embedded in a weighted flower-pot.

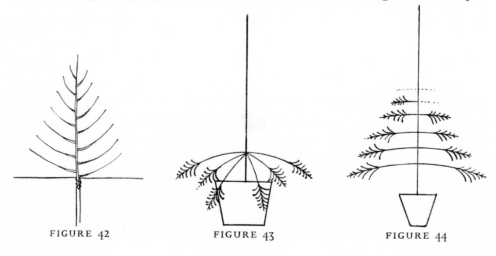

FIGURE 42   FIGURE 43   FIGURE 44

This tree was made from floristry wires, preserved *Adiantum*, beads and feathers.

Above: A country church decorated for a wedding.
Right: An altar vase filled with garden lilac and *Lilium longiflorum*

Table decorations using muslin 'flowers' with small skeleton magnolia leaves and glittered wires. The buds and flowers are made of
nylon organza and silver paper as described on page 137 while the
petals forming the candleholder are alternate layers of organza and
Silsheen ribbon. Glittered wires are used in both decorations to add
the frosted lightness desirable at Christmas time.

It is necessary to cut some of the fronds from the base of the biggest ferns to make the small sprays for the top of the tree. Although very stiff and straight when bought, the plastic ferns can be bent gently into curves, and a tree made entirely of these does resemble, to an astonishing degree, a heavily snow-laden fir tree. When it is decorated very simply with tiny pastel-coloured lights, the effect is arresting and completely in harmony with the Christmas scene.

Where space is available for a green Christmas tree, I think it should be big and gaily decorated in strong colours and lavishly hung with baubles and bells. It should also be in a central position where the family can gather round it and where it can offer a welcome to visiting friends. An entrance hall is the obvious place, but it must be warm enough to make present-opening a pleasant occupation, as gaily-wrapped parcels, when piled beneath a green tree, add considerably to its decoration.

Muslin flowers

These rather nonsensical 'flowers' came about because I was never really satisfied with the introduction of artificial flowers into Christmas arrangements. Plastic flowers were too heavy and unreal amongst the lightness and transparency of the dried and frosted material. By making flowers from suitable fabrics, any colour scheme desired can be carried out and arrangements will be completely in tune with their surroundings. Admittedly, nimble fingers and a modicum of patience are essential but, given these, delicate and lovely results can be achieved. Ordinary organdie, silk or nylon organza, net or any semi-transparent material which is firm enough to

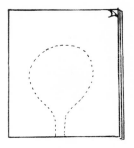

FIGURE 45

FIGURE 46

FIGURE 47

retain its shape is suitable. The petals are cut out by folding the material into several thicknesses as shown in Figure 45, the number and size depending on the type of group envisaged. Usually anything from nine to fifteen petals are required, and they are more effective as flowers if two shades of the same colour are used. The stamens are made by dipping single stub wires first into the glue and then into the glitter for about two or three inches of their length. The stamens can be varied by attaching tiny beads to the tips or they can be bent into different shapes. These are then bound firmly together at a point where the glittering ends, and the remaining wires become the 'stem' of the flower. The petals are attached as shown in Figure 47, and it is important that the stem and petals are held firmly between the first finger and thumb of the left hand while the wire is bound round tightly in one place. If this binding creeps down the stem the petals will not spring from a joint base and the appearance of a flower will then be lost. Finally, the wire stems are bound with strips of crêpe paper to tone with whatever colour scheme is used. The picture facing page 137 shows table decorations made from materials of this kind and it will be seen how large is the scope for invention with glittered wires alone.

The illustration facing page 113 also shows several types of decorations which could be useful at Christmas time. The rather flamboyant 'poinsettias' are made in a similar manner to the muslin flowers but with entirely different material. The ones illustrated are made from red Silsheen ribbon and the petals are long and pointed. Six or seven petals are required for each flower and, as they have to be curved in shape, it is necessary to place a stub wire down the centre back of each petal which is held in place by Sellotape as shown in Figure 48. The stamens are made by rolling small

FIGURE 48   FIGURE 49   FIGURE 50   FIGURE 51

pieces of green crêpe paper between two fingers until they form a little roll. (Figure 49). Silver wire is then bound round each roll to form a stem, and finally half a dozen are bound together to form a bunch of stamens, the tips of which should be touched with yellow paint. The prepared petals are then bound on to the main stem, as described above and shown in Figures 50 and 51, and, when completed, the wired petals are shaped by bending them downwards and slightly backwards to form a remarkably realistic 'poinsettia'. These silken flowers are extremely effective among painted natural material which is in tones of gold or mother-of-pearl, the latter colour being achieved by mixing silver paint with a little gold paint.

The wreath shown in the same illustration is made on folded newspapers, as described on page 127, and decorated with bows of Silsheen ribbon on to which wired sprays of beads and baubles are attached. The long curving tails are made by covering thick wire (such as that used for supporting raspberry canes) with red ribbon and the glittering sprays are also made with wired beads.

The holly-ball tree in the jewelled pot is a festive decoration for any position. The requirements are simple and consist of a small, ordinary flower-pot, a thin bamboo stick, a little Polyfilla, Bostik glue, moss, wire-netting, red ribbon, sprigs of holly and any bits of old jewellery, broken mirrors, Christmas glitter beads and shiny coloured paper that are available. First of all, the stick must be fixed firmly in the pot between four small cross-sticks and a two-inch base of Polyfilla, after which the decoration of the pot can begin. The largest and prettiest piece of jewellery should be chosen for the centre round which the pattern can be built, first covering that portion of the pot with glue. Several rows of different-sized beads can be glued round the rim, and also round the base, while the spaces are filled in with any pieces that seem suitable. (These steps are shown in Figures 52–54.) Although a definite pattern is preferable, it requires a lot of similar

FIGURE 52

FIGURE 53

FIGURE 54

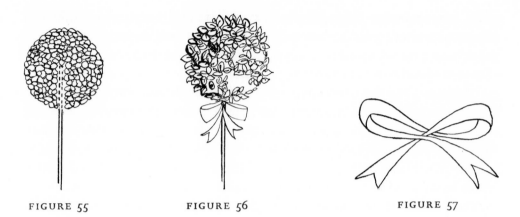

FIGURE 55   FIGURE 56   FIGURE 57

pieces as the sides should match each other, but a completely miscellaneous collection can be worked into a brilliant mosaic and is also extremely effective. The stem is then bound with ribbon which is attached at both ends with Sellotape. The mossed ball is made as described and illustrated on page 117, and then covered with small sprigs of holly which can either be pinned into place with a hairpin-bent wire or mounted on two legs as described in Chapter 2 under 'Mounting flowers', before insertion into the moss. (Figures 55 and 56.) Additional artificial berries can be added if necessary or the tips of some leaves can be touched with glitter. Finally a bow is added and as this is one of the hardest things to achieve successfully, especially with one-sided ribbon, Figure 57 shows how it is done.

The little cones of Christmas baubles make charming table decorations and can be as simple or as ornate as desired. They are made by filling a small vase with Plasticine so that it forms a mound above the rim. A candle can be inserted directly into this, and it is then surrounded in descending circles by beads and baubles, most of which can be stuck directly into the Plasticine or, if they have no wire or stem attached, they can be glued in place.

The fairy-like tree facing page 136 is an example of the type of work which can be done with Christmas material when the rudiments of floristry have been mastered. The tree itself was made of stub wires twisted together to form the curving trunk, while single wires curled round a stone in the manner of roots. These were then painted with a mixture of silver and gold paint and sprinkled with glitter. The leaves were made from sprays of preserved adiantum which were lightly touched with the same mixture of paint, while the birds were made entirely from stub-wires, multi-coloured Christmas beads and a few white feathers.

The foregoing are a few suggestions for those with inventive minds and, let us admit it, a certain amount of time to spare. But they do have the merit of offering possibilities for making gay and unusual decorations which are also remarkably economical.

Evergreens

In many houses the sheer prettiness of frosted decorations may seem out of place, or members of the family, of all ages, may be anxious to help. Then I think evergreens are the answer. Results are achieved quickly and a house is transformed immediately. Children, in particular, love to help at Christmastime but are quickly bored if the decorations take too long. Even evergreens look a little tired if deprived of water, and are apt to shed their leaves, so this type of decoration is best done as late as possible. But there is, perhaps, an added excitement about being busy on Christmas Eve instead of weeks ahead of time, which seems customary these days.

Too often holly and mistletoe are seen stuck indiscriminately behind picture frames or light brackets and festooned round the tops of furniture. Neither show to best advantage when treated in this manner and are often harmful to the walls as the stems of evergreens are generally dirty. On the other hand, it is not difficult to arrange them in such a manner that they are original and festive and harmless to their surroundings.

To achieve perfection with all evergreens it is really necessary to wipe the leaves with a soft cloth as they collect dust and dirt through the seasons. There is unlikely to be time for this at Christmas, but dead wood, and broken or imperfect leaves, should be removed.

Holly and mistletoe

There are endless possibilities with holly, but it is an evergreen which must, to my mind, be kept under control and rigorously pruned of heavy and unnecessary stems before use. It is gay and pretty if tied in small bunches and decorated with bows and streamers of scarlet ribbon. These can be hung anywhere by string loops, and they are an easy decoration for even the youngest member of the family to make. Wreaths or crescents can be made on thick wire or rolled newspaper bound with scarlet ribbon and then decorated with sprays of holly. These are suitable for mantelpieces, or for hanging on doors or, indeed, as wall decorations.

Holly balls hung from a central candelabrum by gay ribbons are unusual and remarkably pretty when seen swinging under the lights. They can be made by tying a handful of moss firmly together with string in the shape of a ball. Small pieces of holly, either on their own stems or, better still, on wire stems, are then pushed into the moss, starting at the top and continuing in circles to the base. It is important that the pieces of holly are all the same size, thereby maintaining an even shape. If the holly is short of berries it is legitimate, I think, to introduce some clusters of artificial berries, as the balls need colour. When variegated holly is available it is helpful to mix the two kinds, as the effect is then lighter. And the whole effect is greatly enhanced if the tips of occasional leaves are varnished and sprinkled with glitter. This, of course, applies to any holly decorations provided you have the time to do it.

Mistletoe, although as integral a part of the Christmas scene as holly, is nevertheless rarely seen in abundance and very often not seen at all. It has a delicate beauty of its own and deserves better treatment than the tight little bunch hung aloft to symbolize the 'kissing bough'. Its grey-green leaves and translucent berries look beautiful arranged with white Christmas roses, and together make a suitable table decoration which is in quiet contrast to the colour and glitter elsewhere but is still in harmony with it. Mistletoe can, of course, also be used for crescents, wreaths or balls in just the same way as holly, but it requires no additional adornment in the way of glitter.

Green decorations

Carefully chosen evergreens can make as beautiful a decoration in winter as any flower arrangement, but one must be selective. Heavy stems must be removed and only perfect foliage retained. Leaves of the bigger evergreens should be arranged so that they face the correct way. In a house where the Christmas decorations are of the traditional green variety, bunches and swags of evergreens are most in keeping. The line of an elegant staircase can be brought into prominence if the newel posts are decorated with trailing bunches of mixed greenery, and swags of ivy, or of laurel or rhododendron leaves, as described and illustrated on page 127, are hung in curves beneath the banister rails. These can be intertwined with ribbons and hung with baubles, or decorated in any manner that is similar to the scheme elsewhere. Swags also look remarkably effective if hung over door lintels with two long ends, of different lengths, left to hang down on either side. These can be intertwined with ribbons and finished off with tassels or bells.

It is probable that some of the foregoing suggestions may sound exaggerated, but Christmas is a time for fantasy when every effort to attain a glittering beauty is to be encouraged. I think that the only qualification should be that we restrict our inventions to decorations which will really adorn our homes and retain the true spirit of Christmas.

II. The Joy of Flowers

For many years people have said to me with envy, 'How lucky you are to work with flowers', and, of course, they have been right. To find a pursuit which increases in interest as time passes is something most of us desire, as boredom is a melancholy state at any age. The pleasure of looking forward is often greater than the realization of joy itself, and the perpetual hope of achieving even a momentary perfection is the factor I have found so absorbing in flower decoration.

Images crowd one's mind to form new ideas, and the seasons merge together in spot-lighting memory on things pertinent to the portrayal of flowers so that each successive day holds out the promise of this will-o'-th'-wisp attainment. I suspect there is a restlessness in my disposition which requires the stimulus of future projects and that others, more serene than I, can live contentedly day by day. But for me, flowers and their arrangement have amply filled this need.

A florist's way of life is not always enviable. Flowers must be bought in the early hours and there are many cold, wet mornings when there is little pleasure in being up while others lie asleep. There are also long days and missed meals because decorations must be finished on time; chilly hands and wet feet because flowers are kept in damp, cool places, and inevitable disappointments when planned arrangements must be completed with substitutes due to the vagaries of price and climate.

The conflicting demands made on the characters of those who work with flowers are, perhaps, more difficult and less understood than anything else. At least a modicum of creative ability is necessary for flower arrangement, which presupposes some artistic talent and a sensitivity towards the medium used, but the decorator must develop a stoic indifference to adverse criticism of, and disinterest in, her most inspired efforts. It would be impossible to please everyone, not only because of differing tastes but also of human failings and, therefore, constructive criticism is both necessary and stimulating. But disapproval, when one has tried one's best, and, even worse, the perfunctory comment of 'quite nice, thank you' are factors in a decorator's life which force upon one a thick-skinned invulnerability which is the antithesis of an artistic temperament.

The rewards, however, far outweigh the hazards. There is delight when one's work gives pleasure. There is always the interest of meeting new people with whom the common topic is flowers, while the continual sight of new places, and of gardens which vie in beauty with each other, gives one opportunities to observe things relative to one's pursuit which are rarely accorded to those in other professions. Anyone who really enjoys flower arrangement must also know the peace which comes with complete absorption when one's mind is swept clean of all but the job in hand. And, because flowers are not inanimate, there is no sense of loneliness. Flowers are 'givers', whatever way they are treated.

I wish I could indicate how long it takes to make flower arrangement an acquired and simplified art, but it has never become that for me. Flowers have a gentle way of reminding one that the ever-varying beauty of their structure keeps them far ahead of the artifices of human presentation. It is only at the beginning that one has real self-confidence, and there is much to be encouraged in this early assurance. Anyone with a real feeling for line and colour can make attractive arrangements without having much knowledge of flowers themselves. In fact, contrary to general opinion, a decorator need not be a horticulturalist any more than a painter, who must be able to mix his paints, need know the chemical processes which are required for their production. But it is, of course, essential to know the varieties of the flowers used and also, in time, to appreciate the subtleties of their character, as otherwise arrangements would lack that touch of sensitivity which can lift them from the mediocre to the great.

I loved flowers and their arrangement long before I had any desire to enquire into the methods of their culture. But interest engenders curiosity, and naturally the more one knows about flowers the more understanding one can be about their portrayal in decoration.

All those who are both gardeners and decorators must suffer at times a mental tug-of-war as to whether flowers show best in the garden or indoors and, space permitting, it is advisable to have a picking garden for the latter purpose. Perversely, this rarely works out right for me; flowers that are intended to be picked in bud are apt to be planted in regimented rows, while the more treasured plants find special places where they can be more generally enjoyed. But there is no need to despoil a garden because these plants provide flowers for indoor decoration, as the judicious gathering of a few stems here and there is rarely noticeable.

The owner of a lovely near-by garden, which has provided so many of the flowers and shrubs illustrated in this book, no longer follows me around with an anxious look when I go to pick for photography sessions or even for large assignments. Both he and his gardener now admit that it is rarely apparent that I have been there at all. This is an inherited garden which has been planted during two generations with rare shrubs and blossoming trees, so that in the spring and autumn, particularly, it is a wealth of beauty for all to see. Magnolias grow in a profusion I have not seen elsewhere, and there is a majestic *M. × soulangiana* 'Lennei' whose branches, laden with chalice-like purple flowers, sweep the ground. This tree is so prolific that I have used long stems in decoration with no apparent depredation to the tree itself.

I find it a source of inspiration to wander round this garden, and many an arrangement has materialized because some flower or shrub has conjured up a picture which is, so fortunately, immediately realizable. There is always some new excitement as the annual pattern of flowering shrubs is not always the same. For instance, the green group facing page 56 came about when I saw the singular green bubbles on a *Dipelta floribunda* shining among the leaves at the back of a shrub border while near by a *Cornus kousa* was covered in neat, pale green flowers.

Through the years the many varieties of philadelphus have grown to such dimensions that arching stems of over six feet can be picked with no noticeable effect on the bush itself, while in some cases varieties have grown together so that cascades of double and single flowers flow out as from the same source. Similarly, a double *Kerria japonica v. flore pleno* has mingled with the more elegant single variety of *K. japonica* itself, thereby suggesting the charm of this mixture in decoration which I have used on many occasions with other yellow flowers.

I had intended originally that the picture to illustrate autumn should be a rich medley of berries, fruit and flowers which would be typical of the year's harvest and the blazing warmth of colour given out before leaves fall. The illustration facing page 81, however, shows that it is fatal to have preconceived ideas when there is a garden in which to wander and unexpected beauties to be found. In this case it was the enormous scarlet heps on a *Rosa moyesii* which tumbled in cascades of arching branches to the ground while, in front of it, bushes of floribunda roses still had flowers in bloom but with dimmed colours, as fading petals hid the brilliance of those still in growth. Suddenly there seemed no necessity for the richness I had planned, as the berries and flowers before me were all the example I required.

I talk of autumn, but my first sense of spring comes in February each year when I see an immense *Cornus mas* covered from summit to ground with tiny, golden-yellow flowers. The faintest breeze sways the twiggy stems on which the flowers are clustered, and the whole effect is as if a mantle of fine yellow lace had been dropped over the bare branches of a spreading tree.

It might appear from my descriptions so far that this is a garden filled with overgrown plants and shrubs, but this, of course, is not the case at all. More recently planted specimen shrubs are there in as much variety as those of greater age, but these must be regarded for the time being as botanical specimens rather than as material for decorative purposes indoors. It is only when a shrub has reached a certain state of maturity that branches can be picked with some assurance of their lasting powers, as it is rare for young growth to last well if cut while still in the tender soft stage.

Recently the owners of this garden gave a dance, for which we had the exciting work of doing the flowers. It was held in the Merchant Taylor's Hall, which has been magnificently restored following bomb damage in the war. I feel it may be helpful to describe this party in some detail, as the problems involved in organizing flower decorations on such a scale are very different from those in one's own home and yet many people now want to do the flowers for their own parties themselves.

On this occasion, with such a wealth of garden plants and shrubs at our disposal, it was desirable that they should be made the main feature of the decorations. But—and this is a matter which is often overlooked—flowers and foliages gathered from a private garden can present unforeseen problems. It is as bad, at times, to have too much material as it is to have too little, and those who are not experienced in cutting flowers and branches for professional decoration can gather much that is of little use, or is in such unnecessary abundance that it is both wasteful in material and in the time taken to sort it out.

It is advisable therefore, in such circumstances, to view the garden beforehand and to find out from the owner or gardener what will be available on the specified date and to make thereafter a list as detailed as a market list for all that is required. For instance, if only a few stems of some particular material are needed it would be a pity to despoil the plant unnecessarily by gathering more than the required amount and, in any case, most flower arrangements look better if arranged on the light side rather than crammed with flowers just because they happen to be available.

The dance was held in late autumn so garden flowers were almost over, but there were coloured leaves and berries in more variety than we had ever seen before. Imagine the material in the group facing page 81 repeated a hundredfold and you will have some idea of the richness at our disposal.

As an early start was necessary for a decoration on this scale it was essential that everything was ready the day before the party. Most of the foliages and berries were gathered several days before, as there was a risk that the glorious peony foliage might have been damaged by a storm and berried branches need judicious pruning and removal of thorns or damaged leaves before use in decoration. This all takes time and could not be left to the last moment when market flowers would have to be prepared.

Although rich autumn tones were the main theme of the decorations, the dark walls of the panelled hall, which was transformed into the ballroom, required light flowers, and here the huge and spreading groups had points of feathery pampas fronds while the design was outlined with pale amber asparagus fern, five or six feet in length, together with immense osmunda ferns which were turning from lime to gold. Golden Auratum

148

lilies and buff-coloured Rayonnante chrysanthemums stood out against a background of cream chrysanthemum spray, while gigantic artichoke leaves gave a central depth to groups which had to be almost architectural in design in view of their immense size.

Sculptured swags of similar coloured flowers hung in loops and drops from the gilded railings of the balcony above, so that the dark and slightly sombre hall was alight with flowers from every angle.

Every room was different. One had a priceless wallpaper where the unusual mingling of flowers in tones of orange, flame, deep blue and silvery pink was repeated in groups of flame kniphofias, 'Super Star' roses, clear, bright pink nerines and blue hydrangea heads. Another room had pale panelled walls with spot-lit niches in which we stood gold dolphins filled with a medley of clashing red flowers, while a third was dramatically outstanding by reason of shining panelling hung with dark portraits which gave the overall impression of tones of ivory fading into deep purple and black. Here, in an ivory Dresden fruit bowl, the arrangement was of fruit and flowers where open 'White Swan' roses and small greenish-white arums mingled with black grapes and aubergines to form a group similar in tone to the portraits above it. Trails of pale ivy, *Hedera helix* 'Chicago', and the unusual marble-like leaves of *Sedum Weinbergii* blended together, by their intermediate shades, the cool white flowers and dark fruit.

Fruit and flowers were also used for the cones which lined the buffet, one of which is shown facing page 112, while groups of reddening leaves, flowers and berries in all the mellow richness of autumn's harmony decorated the entrance hall, the stairs and the long, cloister-like corridor which adjoined the ball-room.

This was a great occasion, attended by members of the Royal Family, and we were prodigal with flowers; but decorations such as these, where a personal element is introduced by the use of the party-giver's own outstanding flowers or foliages, can add considerably to the general success and make such a dance an unforgettable event.

Yet little things can be as memorable. I remember struggling to the top of a wind-swept hill with a heavy mossed circlet of tiny flowers to adorn a font for a baby's christening because no road reached the church and yet such flowers were much desired. Then there was the time I flew to

Scotland for a special decoration when the storm that raged throughout blew the flowers from my hand and yet, somehow, the job was done. And the occasion when a fountain of flowers was to be arranged in the middle of a garden pool but unexpected rains had deepened the water to such an extent that it was necessary to work bare-footed in borrowed shorts as gum-boots were completely submerged.

I recall, too, the laughter shared among colleagues when at the end of two days' arduous collecting of flower donations for a charity ball we found we had a veritable arboretum of bits and pieces in greenery (known to be my speciality) but scarcely a flower at all.

Another great occasion we will always remember was when we were asked to make ponies of white flowers for a Ball held by the Household Brigade Polo Club which was to be attended by the Queen and Prince Philip. The frames were made for us by a group of artists skilled in such work, and then one of us had the bright idea that only shattered carnations would give the right effect of sleek coats. It was a bright idea but the labour involved was monumental. Hundreds of carnations were used, and at one period the work-room looked as if snow had fallen as it was so bestrewn with delicate white petals. But smooth-coated deliciously scented ponies did materialize which proudly took their place in spot-lit niches moments before the ball began.

Important or trivial, the memories remain—flowers and people and places forming together a mental anthology which gains interest with the years and becomes a treasure-house both for reflection and inspiration.

There may be those who consider the arrangement of flowers as a pursuit or hobby is rather inconsequential because it produces little that is of lasting value. But a transitory work of art can be repeated and improved upon, or even conveniently forgotten, and I feel that beauty in any form will always be enjoyed as long as we have eyes with which to see.

For my part I cannot imagine a time when the enjoyment of arranging flowers might pall. The diverse interests which result from it become increasingly absorbing as time passes so that one looks forward

> 'When the feast is laid for a day reborn . . .'

with an eagerness that does not abate with the years.

EAU CLAIRE DISTRICT LIBRARY

Index